BATMAN™
FOREVER

BATMAN™
FOREVER

**Novelization by Alan Grant
Based on a Screenplay Written by
Lee Batchler & Janet Scott Batchler
and Akiva Goldsman**

Batman Created by Bob Kane

Little, Brown and Company
Boston   New York   Toronto   London

To my grandmother, who first introduced me to the wild
and wonderful world of books

First Edition

ISBN 0-316-32418-3
Library of Congress Catalog Card Number: 95-75971

The characters and events in this book are fictitious. Any similarity to real
persons, living or dead, is coincidental and not intended by the author.

10 9 8 7 6 5 4 3 2 1

MAR

Published simultaneously in Canada by Little, Brown & Company (Canada)
Limited and in Great Britain by Little, Brown and Company (UK) Limited

Printed in the United States of America

BATMAN™
FOREVER

Prologue

Driving rain beat against the walls of Arkham Asylum for the Criminally Insane, the howling wind drowning out the shrieks of even its most disturbed inmates. Fiery red lightning cracked the night, throwing the Gothic walls and roofs into sharp relief, like an old sepia photo from a madman's scrapbook.

Chief psychiatrist Dr. Burton's face was tense as he moved down the old hallway. Storms like this really upset his inmates — something to do with the electricity interfering with their brains? he wondered. He filed the thought away, like so many others, to gather dust until it was forgotten. The day-to-day running of the asylum demanded all the time he had.

"Hell of a night, huh, Doc?" the guard greeted Burton

as he stepped through the doorway into the Maximum Security wing.

"Hell's in here," Burton answered quietly.

Hydraulics hissed, the thick riot door slid open, and Burton stepped into a small cell.

A single barred skylight cast the room in pallid moonlight, picking out the solitary figure seated there, back to the door, bound by the wraps and ties of a straitjacket. Outside, lightning flashed, brightening the room momentarily. An instant later, a peal of thunder.

"Mr. Dent . . ." No reply. Burton stepped closer. "Counselor." Still the figure remained silent. Burton took another step.

"Harvey . . ."

Burton leaned forward, touching the man's shoulder. Lightning flashed again as the body whipped round — to reveal an orderly, gagged, bound to the chair with strips of bedsheet.

The motion jerked the thread attached to the ceiling fan control. It whipped into life, picking up speed, winding the sheet tied to it round its wide blades. The body leaped up suddenly, grotesquely, and began to revolve with the fan.

Overhead, twisted iron supports bore testimony to where the skylight had been burned through. He'd escaped!

The hair rose on the back of Burton's neck. For the first time he noticed the madman's scrawl on the wall: THE BAT MUST DIE.

Chapter 1

Gothic towers of granite and glass shimmered golden in the autumn sunset. Cocooned in the comfort of his personal helicopter, billionaire Bruce Wayne watched the news on a small TV screen.

"— in Gotham City last night, ex-district attorney Harvey Dent escaped from Arkham Asylum . . ."

Wayne turned in his seat, the sun's last rays catching his handsome profile. The chopper rose, held steady, then moved into the city. Labyrinthine buildings peeled back one by one as they headed toward the graceful spire of Wayne Enterprises Tower.

The announcer's voice droned on: "Dent was horribly scarred by underworld kingpin Boss Moroni during an indictment hearing two years ago . . ." Wayne's lips set grimly as the announcer's face dissolved to a replay of that courtroom attack.

Again he heard the DA's strident accusations — saw the vial in Moroni's hand as he splashed out its hissing acid. "The resulting left-brain damage transformed Dent into a violent criminal, who launched a grisly crime spree before being captured by the Batman."

Wayne sighed and closed his eyes as the chopper came in to land on the tower pad.

"The solar generator tests are back!" "The mayor's office called!" "Who are you asking to the circus?" "Five minutes to your inspection —" "The President says you left your tennis racquet at the White House!"

A gaggle of voices greeted Bruce Wayne as he stepped into his penthouse office suite. His secretary, Margaret, was closely followed by a half-dozen aides, who thronged round him, bristling papers, waggling pencils, vying for his attention.

He dealt with the first of the requests, and juggled three phone calls simultaneously, but the demands never let up.

"Stop!" Wayne's hand was raised. Everybody froze. Instantly. "Okay," he went on slowly. "Let's all just take a deep breath."

Amid puzzled glances and suspicious nods, he turned

and walked from the room again, chuckling to himself. "I gotta give myself a raise!"

It was dusk outside now, but Wayne's tour of his electronics division was only just beginning. Ranks of workspaces seemed to run to eternity. His usual entourage of junior execs and aides trailing behind him, Wayne followed Fred Stickley, the fussbudget plant manager.

"Your inspections are a departmental highlight," Stickley said fawningly.

"Really?" Bruce shot him a warm, disarming smile. "You all need to get out more!"

Further along the vast line of workstations, a gangling, awkward figure stooped over a desk cluttered with paperwork, games, Rubik's cubes, and dozens of puzzle books all boasting the green-suited caricature of The Guesser. Edward Nygma was working feverishly, welding and soldering and trying out wires in various connections, keeping up a running monologue to himself. "We'll probably be dining at Wayne Manor together," he muttered. "Bruce, could you pass the gravy boat? I forgot — you have people who do that, don't you? A party — in my honor?"

Edward paused, his jaw dropping as if at some horrific realization. He leaned forward, then banged his head against the desk in self-inflicted punishment. "I should have rented a tuxedo! What? One of yours, Bruce? Why not? We're the same size."

The wall of his small cubicle was plastered with photos of Bruce Wayne, clipped from newspapers and magazines. Bruce was Edward's hero.

He looked up at the sound of an approaching commotion. "It's him!"

Bruce was striding up the corridor, a posse of people clustering after him as if he were some eastern guru. A shadow crossed Stickley's face. He'd seen Ed Nygma on the fringe of the group. Hurriedly, Stickley took Bruce's arm and tried to steer him away.

But he was too late. Edward had pushed through the throng and was standing directly in front of Bruce, taking his hand as he gushed, "Nygma. Edward Nygma. You hired me, Mr. Wayne." In a lower voice he added: "Well, we've never actually met, but your name was on the hire slip."

Bruce looked down at his hand, still firmly held in the ungainly man's grip. "I'm gonna need that hand back, Ed."

Nygma started, then let the hand go apologetically. "I'm sorry. It's just that . . . you're my idol." He darted a meaningful glance at Stickley. "Only, some people have been trying to keep us apart."

"What's on your mind, Mr. Nygma?" Bruce asked.

Edward smiled. "What's on all our minds? Brain

waves. The future of Wayne Enterprises is brain waves!" He paused, acutely aware that every eye was on him, every voice was stilled except for a single snigger — Stickley's.

"Go ahead, Edward," Bruce said softly.

"I knew you'd understand!" Edward gestured to his untidy cubicle. On the worktop stood a TV set, jury-rigged to transceivers, diodes, and tangled wires running to two elaborate, futuristic headbands. "My invention beams any TV signal directly into the human mind. By stimulating neurons — manipulating brain waves, if you like — this device creates a fully holographic image that puts the audience inside the show. Become a member of your favorite TV family. Laugh with them. Cry with them."

Edward paused before going on. "Why be brutalized by an uncaring world? My Remote Encephalographic Stimulator Box will give Joe Q. Public a realm where he is king!" He looked round at Bruce. "Not that *you'd* need it, of course. Witty. Charming. But for the lonely, the —"

"Paranoid?" Stickley broke in cruelly. "The psychotic?"

Edward went on as if the other man hadn't spoken. "The Box will change lives! You will become King of Electronics. Wayne Enterprises will spearhead a technological entertainment revolution." His expression was hangdog as he looked at Bruce again. "I just need a bit of additional funding for human trials. Let me show you . . ."

7

Bruce suddenly caught a light out of the corner of his eye. Through the window he saw the Bat-Signal beaming bright against the night clouds. Many had seen it, but few knew of its purpose: to advise Gotham City's own vigilante that the police needed his help.

"Let me see your schematics on all this, Ed," Wayne began hurriedly, but Nygma was in full flow, and in no mood to be stopped.

"We'll be full partners in this, Bruce. What talks we'll have, late into the night. I'm not so accustomed to business travel, so go easy on me. Look at us. Two of a kind!"

Bruce's eyes darted again toward the Bat-Signal. "Call Margaret. She'll set something up."

He turned to leave, but Edward grabbed his arm. "Wait! You can't go," he cried. Then sudden rage overwhelmed his desperation. "Don't leave me! My invention! I need you!"

Bruce dislodged the hand on his arm without expression. "I'm sorry, Edward. I'm sure you mean well. But I have always felt technology should help us live our lives, not escape them. Tampering with people's brain waves is mind manipulation. It raises too many question marks."

He turned away. "Factory looks great, folks. Keep up the good work."

Then he was gone, leaving Edward Nygma glaring balefully after him. "You were supposed to understand." His eyes darkened with growing obsession. "I'll *make* you understand!"

If Bruce Wayne had been able to hear the quiet menace in those words, he might have thought again.

Bruce moved quickly, entering his sumptuous office. "Lock," he snapped, and as the door automatically sealed itself, he sloughed off his playboy industrialist image the way a snake sheds its skin. Only faster.

Dropping into a soft leather chair, he uttered the word "Capsule." Immediately the seat dropped, sliding quickly into a sleek one-man transport capsule. It had cost his company a fortune to install this new and highly secret elevator route, one that was used by only one man.

The capsule dropped like a stone, its air brakes cushioning it against impacting the bottom of the tube. From there, a tight tunnel stretched off into the distance, and the capsule shot through it at near-supersonic speed.

Inside the capsule, Bruce flicked on a communication screen. "Alfred —" he began, but the face of his trusted retainer — his best and only real friend — was already there on the screen.

"I saw the signal, sir," the butler explained. "All is ready."

He was waiting as the capsule shot out of the tunnel's end and into its special docking bay in the Batcave — the vast, secret underground cavern beneath Wayne Manor. Bruce stepped out, the sense of urgency about him in sharp contrast to his earlier relaxed pose. Quickly, he took the costume Alfred had laid out for him, and slipped into it with practiced speed. Leggings, tunic, boots, cape, gloves . . . just clothes, items of apparel . . . until he put them on.

A small shiver ran up Alfred's spine, the way it always did when he saw his master take on the potent, terrifying role he played.

For Bruce Wayne was the Batman, Gotham's Darknight Avenger.

He slid into the cockpit of the car that waited in its bay. Fifteen feet long, the sleek black Batmobile boasted the kind of horsepower that would haul a tank, with every electronic safety and traction device known to automotive science . . . and a few that were unknown outside this very cave.

"I suppose I couldn't talk you into taking along a sandwich?" Alfred asked drily.

"I'll get drive-thru," Batman replied. "Go!"

The voice-activated engine came to life, selected first gear, and took off. Under a series of support arches, the car picked up speed, the white fusion-glow of the engine turning blue-white, and then translucent blue. The single batlike wing folded back in two as the car became a stealth bullet.

Ahead of him was a solid cave wall. But the amazing machine never faltered — plunging straight through the hologram, then through the trees on the other side, out onto a forest track. A very expensive precaution, but the most secure way to maintain his privacy.

Batman's foot pressed pedal to metal, and the mighty machine shot forward, speeding toward the twinkling lights of Gotham City.

Chapter 2

The Bat-Signal was plainly visible from the twenty-second floor of the Second Bank of Gotham, a huge oval of light and shade blazing steadily into the night sky. A silver dollar flipped up into the air, spinning over and over, momentarily blocking out the signal. Like an omen, Harvey Dent thought. Only, he wasn't Harvey Dent any longer. On his criminal sprees, he called himself Two-Face, in honor of his appalling injuries.

"Counting on the winged avenger to rescue you from evil, old chum?" Two-Face grinned, and turned the un-marked, handsome side of his face toward the bank guard lying on the floor at his feet. The guard's wrists and ankles were bound securely, fear written large on his face. "*We* most certainly are."

It took the guard a moment to figure out who he meant

by "we." Harvey Dent's entire personality had been traumatized by the acid attack, and he always referred to himself in the plural.

"You gonna kill me?" The guard's voice was thick with terror.

Two-Face tapped the guard's hearing aid, considering. "Maybe. Maybe not. You could say we're of two minds on the matter." He thrust his silver dollar under the guard's nose. "Suppose we flip for it?" The upper side of the dollar shone in mint perfection. "One man is born a hero, his brother a coward," Two-Face began. "Babies starve, politicians grow fat. And why is this? Heredity? Environment? Fate? No, my friend. It's down to luck. Blind, simple, idiot, doo-dah luck. The random toss of the great celestial coin is the only true justice. Triumph or tragedy, joy or sorrow. Life — or dare we say it —" He turned the coin, showing the guard the flip side — which, like half his face, bore deep, disfiguring scars — before ending softly: "Death."

His thumb straightened, sent the gleaming coin spinning into the air. The guard watched it, as if hypnotized. He knew Two-Face's modus operandi only too well from the tabloids. Turned from good to evil, the villain could make no decision unless it was approved by the coin — blind fate's decision.

The coin tumbled through the air, landing on the floor close to the guard's sweating face. The unblemished side lay faceup. The coin had decided life.

13

"Fortune smiles upon you, my friend." Two-Face winked, and the guard gave an involuntary sob of relief. "Besides, live bait is always best for any trap!"

Two-Face snapped his fingers. Several of his thuggish gang moved to grab the hapless guard, lifting him bodily off the floor and bearing him away.

One of the other gang members sneered. "Too many witnesses. We shoulda just killed him!"

As soon as he'd said it, the man realized he should have remained silent. This was his first night on the Two-Face gang, but his fellows had warned him: Never question the boss. And that meant, never question the coin's decision.

Two-Face flipped it high now, catching it with well-practiced ease on the back of his hand. The scarred face was up.

Suddenly savage, Two-Face shot his hand out, pinning the hireling's throat to the wall. Slowly he turned his face, the gruesome left side emerging from the shadows, its tortured flesh a hideous mass of red scar tissue.

"You stinking piece of virus-breeding rat droppings! Did you question our coin?" His voice was loaded with menace as he caught the man across the face with a painful backhand slap. "Never," he began, and each word was punctuated by another slap, "never argue with us! Got it?"

"Anything you say, boss," the thug rasped, and sank to the floor in silent gratitude as the blows ceased.

Down on the streets, police wagons lined up. SWAT teams waited coolly, used to the long hours of negotiation that might be necessary before they were ordered into sudden action. Police spotlights cleaved the air, casting the Second Bank's art deco façade into bright relief.

Police Commissioner James Gordon stood at a street corner, waiting. He lit his third cigarette, the match's light revealing a face that had seen it all, yet had still stayed human. He glanced briefly at the beautiful, professionally dressed young woman standing by him. Gordon had dealt with Two-Face before — he knew the perils of dealing with the obsessed maniac. That's why he'd asked Dr. Chase Meridian in on this one. She was an expert on maniacs.

High above them, on one of the pedestrian bridges that snaked between the buildings, the Batmobile screeched to a halt, and another expert leaped quickly out.

The Bat-Signal was obscured, flowed for a moment into the shape of Batman's cape, as the Dark Knight leaped down past the signal, landing lightly face to face with Chase.

"Hot entrance," she said softly.

Batman turned to Gordon, all business. "Two-Face?"

The police chief nodded. "Two guards down. He's holding the third one hostage. We didn't see this one coming."

"We should have," Chase put in, and both men looked at her. "The Second Gotham Bank —"

"— on the second anniversary of the day I captured him," Batman finished for her.

"How could Two-Face resist?" She held out her hand, and Batman shook it briefly. "I'm Chase Meridian. I —"

"— specialize in dual personalities. Abnormal psychology," Batman cut in. "I've read your work."

"I'm flattered. Not every girl makes a super hero's night table."

Gordon glanced up at the building above. "Can we reason with him? There are innocent people in there."

Chase shook her head. "Won't do any good. He'll slaughter them without thinking twice."

"Right," Batman agreed. "A trauma powerful enough to create an alternate personality leaves the victim —"

"— in a world where normal rules of right and wrong no longer apply." Chase paused, and looked keenly at Batman. "Like you, I could write a heck of a paper on a grown man who dresses like a flying rodent!"

"Bats aren't rodents, Dr. Meridian."

She looked down. "Call me Chase. By the way, do *you* have a first name? Or do I just call you Bats?"

She turned back to him, expecting an answer. But he was gone.

Suddenly a titanic boom rocked the night.

Police searchlights swiveled, realigned, and went racing up the face of the bank building. Outside the twenty-second floor, a giant wrecking ball slung beneath a helicopter swung again toward the building wall.

Inside, Two-Face grinned. "Let's start this party with a bang!" He didn't even flinch as the wall behind him exploded, remaining totally unfazed as the wrecking ball crashed into the room and missed him by inches. He liked precision planning.

In the moment's stillness that followed the crash of destruction, Two-Face heard the sharp ding that announced an elevator had arrived. "Punctual," he said drily. "Even for his own funeral."

He and his six gunsels whirled, bringing their machine guns up, fingers already squeezing the triggers. The noise was deafening as a hail of armor-piercing bullets from the massed guns punched holes in the bank of elevator doors, chewing lumps out of the interiors, shredding anyone inside.

The thugs closed in, eager for the kill, as the perforated elevator doors opened to reveal . . . empty shafts.

Before any of them could react, Batman flew out of the center shaft, feet first, sending the thugs scattering. Too fast to follow, his hands crossed to his Utility Belt, each hand jerking free one of the tools he employed in his work. Sworn never to use a firearm or take a life, he had been forced to invent other ways of dealing with the criminals who infested his city.

An air-powered Bat-pistol sent a mass of hyper-adhesive goo onto the closest two villains' feet, and they sprawled to the floor, helpless as the rapidly hardening glue held them fast. Batman's other hand sent a spinning bolo on its way; its tiny whirling cables circled a third villain, bringing him crashing down.

He took the fourth and fifth thugs out with a series of savage karate kicks.

Down the hall, the final thug unfolded his arms to reveal two spike-covered gloves. Screaming some martial arts threat, he barreled toward the vigilante. Batman held his ground, eyes unblinking under the cowl.

A heartbeat before contact with those lethal spikes, Batman sidestepped. The howling villain hurled past him and plummeted down the empty elevator shaft behind, his voice quickly fading. He hit the top of the elevator car with a thud, miraculously sustaining only minor injuries.

Batman caught a glimpse of movement far down the hall, and saw Two-Face disappear round a corner. He gave chase, running round the same corner to discover himself in a large vault area where a massive safe stood, its door gaping open. Inside, Batman saw the bound and gagged guard, writhing and mumbling in desperate incoherence.

He was almost certain the safe was a trap — and yet he had to free the guard. Stepping into the narrow vault, he cut the man's bonds, then tore off the tape that sealed his mouth.

"It's a trap!" the guard yelled, but the safe door was already slamming closed with a hollow clang.

"Good evening, Mr. Bat." Batman didn't look for the hidden speaker that brought Two-Face's words. His mind was already racing, turning over all the possibilities. "Your mission, should you choose to accept it," Two-Face went on, "is simple. Die!"

The safe jerked, the sudden violent motion hurling Batman and the guard to the floor. It shuddered forward, metal scraping on concrete.

Outside, chains latched onto the vault and were yanked taut, dragging it across the floor toward the hole in the wall made by the wrecking ball. Above the bank, a Blackhawk helicopter revved its mighty rotors, and a giant winch steadily hauled the safe-chains over pulleys toward the chopper's waiting cargo hatch.

Beside the pilot, Two-Face laughed into a microphone. "Two years ago, you abandoned us to that so-called asylum. Happy anniversary! And for your dying pleasure, we're serving the very same acid that made ours truly the men we are today!"

Inside the safe, Batman and the aghast guard watched as small spigots attached to the walls began spitting out boiling red acid. Then they fought for balance as the chains dragged the safe out of the building and it dropped, briefly, before jerking taut and dangling there.

"Know the combination?" Batman asked, glancing at the massive lock. Acid hit the metal floor, hissing and smoking.

"No!" The guard scrambled up a wall of cash drawers, desperate to escape the bubbling flood that started to fill the safe. "Can't you blow open the door?" He covered his face from the fumes.

"Acid's flammable. We'd be incinerated." Batman steepled his legs, feet pressing against opposite walls to give him some elevation. Acid burned the end of his drooping cape.

He reached out and grabbed the guard's hearing aid. "I need to borrow this!" He held it up to the door and began working at the safe's combination lock.

He could tell they were rising, being pulled into the air outside the building. He'd deal with that when the time came! His fingers flew over the lock combination, desperately racing against the clock as the ever-increasing flood of acid started to lick at the soles of his boots.

Again, Two-Face's voice filled the safe. "Once we were allies, bound by a passion to fight evil."

The guard wiped sweat from his forehead, knocking off his glasses. They fell, turning molten in a heartbeat.

"Know what we've learned?" Again that taunting, cruel voice. "Passion burns."

The sprays turned to geysers, a stream of acid spurting in. "Burn, Batty, burn!"

Just then the final tumbler on the lock clicked open. Batman threw open the door, grabbing the jamb in one hand and the guard in the other, then swinging out onto the safe's top . . . as a torrent of hissing acid streamed below his feet.

As the Blackhawk slowly rose, the safe came closer to the top of the tower. Batman fired a Batarang into the building wall as an anchor, and attached the Batline to the safe. He palmed his Utility Belt and a laser torch snapped into his glove. Then he reached up, grabbing the chain with his free hand.

"Hang on," he yelled.

"What?" It was all the guard could do to take in what was happening, sights and sounds a blur to his deprived senses.

He was vaguely aware of the panoramic nightscape, the amazing view, as he clung for dear life to the top of the safe.

Batman hit the chain just above the safe with the flare torch, vaporizing the sturdy links. Holding onto the chain, he swung up behind the chopper as the vault — the guard clinging grimly to it — swung like a pendulum on its anchor line, arcing straight for the hole in the bank wall from which it had been pulled.

It flew back in through the hole, slid across the floor, and slammed safely back into place . . . before the bewildered eyes of Commissioner Gordon, Chase Meridian, and an entire investigating SWAT team.

In midair, Batman scrambled up the dangling winch chain toward the open cargo hatch. Two-Face's smile had vanished as he glared out of the side of the chopper. Seething, he grabbed the controls from the pilot. "He wants to play? Fine. Let's play!"

Two-Face hauled back on the throttle, and the chopper shot into the night sky like a rocket.

Batman hung on for grim life as he was whipped around on the end of the chain. As they circled over the harbor area, the chopper started to drop.

Ahead, Batman saw the giant neon WELCOME TO GOTHAM CITY sign that straddled the harbor. Next second they were plunging through it in an explosion of glass and neon stars.

Satisfied his task was done, Two-Face relinquished the controls to his pilot, and went back to the hold. Beneath, the chain dangled. "Ah, to finally be rid of that pointy-eared, steroid-eating, rubber-suited, cross-dressing night rat . . . !"

The pilot's jaw dropped as a familiar black cape fell down across his Plexiglas windshield. "Uh, boss —" he began.

Two-Face spun, drawing his machine pistol, firing in one smooth movement. The spray of bullets blew out windshield and pilot alike. Batman had already gone.

The chopper dived, out of control. Two-Face staggered to the pilot's chair and wrested free the corpse — but Batman's fist smashed through the side window into his jaw.

"You need help, Harvey." Batman was standing on one

of the struts, trying to climb in the open side. "Give it up!"

Two-Face's boot thudded into him, but Batman pulled himself back up and grabbed the madman's foot. The chopper lurched dizzyingly, the night cityscape spinning round them like a kaleidoscope.

"We spent two years in Arkham planning your demise. There's only one way out of this waltz. One of us dies!"

"I won't kill you, Harvey."

Batman had him by the throat, and Two-Face screamed: "Batman doesn't kill? Liar! *You're* a killer, too!"

Somehow his words seemed to shake Batman, as he tried to grasp what his onetime ally meant. The distraction was all that Two-Face needed. He smashed Batman across the face, and the grim avenger fell from sight.

The chopper was careening toward Lady Gotham, the massive bronze statue at the gateway to the city's harbor. Beneath it, clinging to a strut, teeth set against the extreme stress his body had experienced, was Batman.

Two-Face locked the steering control on its deadly course. Batman, exerting every muscle to its utmost, fought to hoist himself back into the chopper through the open side — just in time to see his foe dive out the cargo hatch. "Goodbye, old pal." Two-Face grinned. "Glad to see you go!"

Batman stared in frozen disbelief as his archenemy hurtled toward the dark water below. There was a sudden flurry of expanding color caught in Lady Gotham's light-house beam, and a parachute opened over Two-Face.

Then the chopper plunged into the statue, exploding violently against the side of the massive bronze head. A tremendous fireball split the night as Batman fell, eyes closed.

As the world spun and his descent quickened, memories flashed in Batman's mind. Images as sharp as life.

The light from a single streetlight. His parents, Thomas and Martha Wayne, shot dead, robbed of life and love in an instant by the power of the gun. Young Bruce watches, the horror of that night etched in his soul forever.

Roses fall to the street from a woman's hand. A boy runs through a storm, a book clutched in his hands. Falling . . . falling . . . down a narrow stone chute. The cave beneath . . .

A bat — huge and evil, and screeching like a banshee.

And over everything, Two-Face's words: "You're a killer, too."

Then his eyes opened and Batman plunged into the harbor waters. Ripples spread, then stilled before his cowl broke the surface. Gasping for breath, he stared up at the night sky.

Where the chopper had exploded, Lady Gotham's beautiful face now burned in the night, one side melted and warped and grotesque.

Two-Face had won the first round.

Chapter 3

More than a dozen blocks from the harbor, Wayne Enterprises was closed for the night. Inside, the hundreds of offices and workstations were empty and in darkness . . . save for one.

Edward Nygma sat hunched over his desk, working expertly on the headband attached to his invention. Sweat beaded on his brow, and he mumbled furiously to himself: " 'Too many questions! Too many question marks!' "

He glanced at the photos of Bruce Wayne adorning his wall. "I'll show you!"

"What the devil is going on here?" Stickley stood before the cubicle, distinctly unhappy. "I told you after Mr. Wayne left — this project is terminated. I'm calling Security!"

Lips pursed, he turned to go — and Edward cracked him brutally on the head with a coffeepot.

Stickley awakened to find himself strapped into a swivel chair. Edward had donned one of the electronic headbands, and now he placed the other on Stickley's head. The TV monitor with a Box atop it was running a fishing show, Stickley noted incongruously as Edward spoke: "This won't hurt a bit. At least, I don't think it will."

He reached for the toggle on the power source. A green glow emanated from the screen, enveloping the disbelieving Stickley. In the heart of the glow, like a miniature of real life, a small holographic representation of the fisherman reeled in a prize bass.

Stickley's heart pounded. It was like actually being there! The fisherman's catch flopped wetly in his face — then the figures began to waver and tremble.

"Losing resolution," Edward snapped. "More power!"

He threw a switch. Sparks flew and circuits sizzled. Overload! A white beam shot from the Box, arcing straight to Stickley's headband. Then it backfired through the machine into Ed's headband.

Both men screamed.

Stickley's eyes dulled, glazing over — but for Edward, the effect seemed to be the opposite. He felt invigorated — thrusting — dynamic. His eyes gleamed with a sudden lust for power, as he briefly realized what was happening to him . . . and he stepped over that fine line between sanity and madness.

"Ed Nygma, come on down," he said in his best gameshow host voice. "You're the next contestant on *Brain Drain*. What have we got for him, Johnny?"

His voice went into hypermode. "Stickley, I've had a breakdown! I mean a breakthrough! I'm smarter. I'm a genius! A gaggle of geniuses! I am experiencing a saturation of the cerebrum!"

Again his voice changed, now sounding like a short-order cook's. "Yo, Charlie, gimme an order of Brain Fry. Hold the neurons!"

Seized with awesome power, Edward got to his feet, paced, thrust his face close to Stickley's. "Riddle me this, Fred. What is everything to someone and nothing to everyone else? Your mind, of course! And now mine pumps with the power of yours!"

He began to sing, loudly. "I'm sucking up your IQ, vacuuming your cortex, feeding off your brain!"

At last he turned the machine off. The white beam shorted, sputtered, and went out.

"Fred, you were a wonderful appetizer. But now I yearn for a meal of substance. The main course!" Edward's eyes lit up. "Ah, to taste the mind of a hero, a nobleman, a poet! What a rush!"

Stickley's eyes swam into focus. "What . . . happened?"

"A surprising side effect," Edward told him. "While you were mesmerized by my 3-D television, I utilized your neural energy to grow smarter. And yet, now that my beam is off, your intelligence — as it were — has returned to normal, with no memory of my cerebral siphon!"

Stickley snarled with disgust. "Bruce Wayne was right, you demented, unethical toad! It *is* mind manipulation! I'm reporting you to the FCC, the AMA, the police, the federal government! You're going to court — to jail — to a mental institution for the rest of your twisted little life!" His face contorted with anger. "But first and foremost, Nygma, you are fired! Fired!"

"I don't think so." Edward gave the chair a hefty shove, sending it careening across the slick floor. Stickley was powerless to do anything because of the straps that bound him. There was an almighty crash as the chair burst through the window and teetered on the edge of the building. The long wire from the Box to Stickley's headband was taut, the only thing keeping him balanced there.

For an instant, the terror in his heart died as he saw Edward come toward him. The man was going to save him!

But Edward was only interested in the headband. "Fred. Babe. *You* are fired. Or should I say . . . terminated?"

He pulled the invention from Stickley's head and sent his ex-boss crashing to his death.

He hurried back to his booth and stared at the photos of

Bruce on the wall. "Question marks, Mr. Wayne?" he hissed. "My work raises too many question marks?"

In a frenzy, he began ripping the photos from the wall. "Let me ask *you* some questions, Mr. Smarter-Than-Thou!" He smashed the framed magazine cover on the floor. "Why are you so debonair? Successful? Richer than God?" He stomped spitefully on the picture. "Why should you have it all and not me?"

Pulverized glass ground into the floor beneath his heel, as he imagined he might do soon with his ex-idol's face.

Fleeting images flicker by. Once again comes a scream. Gunshots. Roses fall to the pavement. A young boy stands staring into the Wayne Manor living room at the wake in progress there. Two coffins rest amid the mourners. Thomas and Martha Wayne. His parents.

Dead leaves whip across the floor. Small hands touch a leather-bound book. The wind blows out two flickering candles.

The boy runs through stormy darkness, the book clutched in his hands. He slips. A sinkhole.

A fall down a narrow stone chute, and then he's in the cave. The giant monarch bat screeches toward him, fangs bared as if to feed. And over it all, Two-Face's voice: "You're a killer, too."

Bruce Wayne lay in bed, trying to blink away the images.

Just then, welcoming sunlight, rich like autumn gold, streamed into the room as Alfred drew the curtains.

"The dreams again, sir?" the butler asked.

"I've no time for dreams," Bruce lied. "Status?"

"The computer has been scanning the emergency bands all night. No sign of Two-Face."

"He'll be back."

Bruce sat up, and Alfred couldn't help noticing the fresh bruises on his side. "What a marvelous shade of purple," he said sarcastically. "Really, sir, if you insist on trying to get yourself killed each night . . ." He stooped to pick the carelessly discarded Bat-costume from the floor. He sighed imperceptibly as he saw the rips, dents, and punctures in it, then continued: ". . . would it be a terrible imposition to take better care of your equipment?"

"Then you'd have nothing to complain about."

"Hardly a worry, sir." Alfred held out a robe to Bruce, then told him: "I have the videotape you requested from Arkham Asylum."

Bruce stuck the tape in his machine, frowning as he watched a video case file on Harvey Dent.

Ten minutes later, he'd learned nothing new and was about to switch off during a Dent interview, when he heard the voice on the screen distinctly say: "I'll find a land where light is shadow and freaks are kings. You're a killer, too, Bruce."

Stunned, Bruce hit reverse and watched the clip again.

This time there was no addition. He'd completely imagined that last line.

He flipped to the television news channel and saw Lady Gotham's scarred and twisted face. "— city should charge Batman with felony landmark destruction," a voice was saying. "His vigilantism is a plague on Gotham!"

Sighing, Bruce moved over to a high-tech exercise machine, setting it for maximum resistance and storming into an invigorating workout.

"You know what Chase said to Batman last night?" he asked Alfred between push-ups. "She practically accused him of being crazy!"

Alfred nodded sagely. "Perhaps the lady is just what the doctor ordered!"

"Alfred," Bruce said, a note of urgency in his voice, "why did I become Batman?"

"To avenge your parents. To protect the innocent. To fight crime."

"Of course," Bruce agreed. "But there's something else. What was I doing outside the night of my parents' wake? What sent me running into the storm?"

Alfred shook his head as Bruce moved on to another exercise. They'd had this conversation many times before. "I don't know, sir."

"I remember racing through the fields," Bruce continued. "Falling into the cave. Those fangs. That breath. But there was something else. Something I was running away from. I just can't remember . . ."

The phone rang, and seconds later Bruce switched the machine off as Alfred called: "It's Commissioner Gordon, sir. There's been an accident at Wayne Enterprises!"

"Why, oh why?" Edward Nygma was putting on what he thought was a grief-stricken performance. With increased brain power, however, increased acting talent wasn't guaranteed. "Two years, working in the same office, shoulder to shoulder . . . and then this!"

He broke off, passing a handwritten note to the executive who faced him. "I found this in my cubicle. You'll find the writing matches his exactly, as does sentence structure and spelling."

He sobbed again. "I couldn't possibly continue here. The memories! I'll just get my things!"

Nygma ducked into his cubicle, heaped the Box and bits and pieces of his fantastic invention into the basket of a Wayne Enterprises bicycle, and slipped out a side door to avoid the cops at the front. Gordon and Wayne himself were headed into the building, and he took pains to evade them.

Inside, Bruce paused by a security console and hit a button. "This is last night's security log," he told the commissioner. Onscreen, they saw Fred Stickley scribble a suicide note. Then he turned, ran toward the giant window, and leaped explosively through it.

Gordon shrugged. "Looks cut and dried."

A uniformed cop walked over and gave the commissioner a note. "Definitely suicide," Gordon announced after he'd read it. "Thanks for your help, Bruce. We'll be in touch."

Gordon headed for the exit, while Bruce went to his office. His secretary, Margaret, followed him in.

"Make sure Stickley's family gets full benefits, Margaret."

She made a note in her pad. "Gossip Gerty and the gossip columnists have called a record thirty-two times," she reported. "If they don't know soon who you're taking to the charity circus, the world is surely going to end!"

Bruce noticed a plain envelope on his desk. Warily, he picked it up. "What's this?"

Margaret shrugged. "I don't know. I didn't see anyone."

"No postmark. No stamp," Bruce muttered as he slit the envelope open. He took out the note and read from it:

" 'If you look at the numbers on my face, you won't find thirteen anyplace.' "

Margaret frowned. "I'm sorry?"

"It's a riddle," Bruce told her. "Numbers upon my face, no thirteen . . . a clock."

Margaret's frown deepened. "Who's sending you riddles?"

He glanced again at the note. A photo of Bruce was accompanied by a jumble of letters cut from magazines and newspapers. It was signed with only a question mark. Not the work of a sane mind.

Bruce's eyes narrowed. He had a bad feeling about this.

The whole of Harvey "Two-Face" Dent's life had been taken over by his obsession with duality, a tragic manifestation of the pain and trauma he'd suffered when his face and brain were irrevocably burned.

Even his hideout fitted the theme. The long, low room was divided neatly down the center. On one side — his normal, "good" side — stood the contents of an ordinary apartment: couch, table, chairs, everything neat and orderly. But the other side . . . ! Imagine Frankenstein's monster having a nightmare, and that only partly summed it up. Evil, dark furnishings and sharp metal lined the side paralleling the dark side of Harvey's persona.

The girl he called Spice sat on Two-Face's scarred side. Dressed in tight leather, her lipstick outrageous ruby, she stroked the muzzle of a black Doberman as she smiled at her boss. "Oh, you are most obscene, my frightful grotesque," she told him.

"Don't listen to her!" Spice's sister, Sugar, looking dazzling and innocent in pristine white lace, nuzzled up to Two-Face's handsome side. "You're every girl's dream."

Two-Face shook his head. "Too many bats to fry to think about fun. We wanna take him apart limb from hyperextended limb. Feel his bones crunch in our hands.

Beat him until he's as black and blue as that ridiculous rubber suit of his!"

He'd been seated in the "bad" side of the room, but now he stepped over into what he thought of as Sugarland. His demeanor instantly changed, became more reasoning and calm.

"On the other hand," he said, "perhaps something slow, a delicious incursion of despair, a campaign to shatter his psyche and bring him crumpling to his knees."

He wandered into Spiceland. "Why wait? Rupture his organs! Shatter his spine!"

Absentmindedly, he paced back into Sugarland. "Simple murder? It's just too darn simple. We need a plan."

Then over into Spiceland once again. "Yes. Something senseless, brutal, savage, violent."

He strolled back into Sugarland, adding: "Yet witty!"

Chapter 4

The Criss Cross Cleaners had survived in Gotham's Chisholm district for nearly seventy years before finally giving up the battle as the neighborhood steadily declined. All that remained of them now was the giant crossword puzzle ad that was painted over the entire side of the apartment building where they'd been located. Letters were missing and much of it was scrawled with gang graffiti, a wry reminder of better days, now long gone.

Inside, in his dirty, cramped basement apartment, Edward Nygma hammered and pounded and soldered. The place was a nightmare, a jumble of every kind of electric and electronic junk and gadgetry under the sun. In one corner, an old circus booth contained a life-sized mannequin of the green-clad quiz-magazine star, The Guesser.

Eventually, Edward gave a triumphant cry and hurled the old electronic headband into the trash can. Its replacement looked better, worked better, and promised to deliver even more neural power.

He looked up at the old mannequin, irritated by the stupid grin on its face. He'd kept it around for years, a present from his grandad before he died. "Guess what, Guesser? *I'm* the guy with all the answers!"

The mannequin glared back at him with, as Edward imagined, dumb insolence. "Stop staring at me!" he snapped, lashing out with the high-tech cane he'd been constructing, snapping off the dummy's head in one swift move.

Now that his invention was finally perfected, Edward was ready to move into the big time. His lip curled in a sneer as he looked around the tiny apartment. "These digs barely achieve minimum specs for a chicken pen, much less residential accommodation!" He sniffed the air, his newly increased intelligence surprising even him. "And the air! Carbon molecules outproportion oxygen by twenty-three percent more than the situational norms!" He groaned aloud. "Please! I can't rule the world from here!"

He clambered up on an overflowing shelf, struggling upright so he could reach the tiny skylight above. His voice switched to that of a blustery executive: "Boys, I want one of these babies in every home." Now affecting a presidential drawl: "It's the new information superhigh-way and I'm in the carpool lane!" An ad-man: "From their brains to the TV to my brain, with no commercial inter-ruptions!"

His head smashed through the window at sidewalk level, and Edward grinned as he watched the feet of passersby.

"There are seven million brains in the Naked City . . . and they'll all be mine!"

Bruce Wayne was disappointed when he finally met Dr. Chase Meridian the next day. When he'd seen her before, he was in his Batman guise, and he knew he hadn't imag-ined the sparks that flew between them. But she seemed to have little interest in plain Bruce Wayne. He was in her temporary office at the Gotham Municipal Police com-plex, showing her the patchwork riddles he'd received. A second one had been delivered to the manor.

"The first answer is a clock," she said, frowning. "But this? 'Tear one off and scratch my head. What once was red is black instead.'"

"A match," Bruce told her. He'd already solved it. He tapped his fingers absentmindedly as he watched her.

"Psychiatrists make you nervous?" she asked.

He flashed her a dazzling smile. "Just beautiful ones."

Chase rolled her eyes. "The infamous Wayne charm. Does it ever shut off?"

"You should see me at night," he said enigmatically.

He turned away and examined the volumes on her bookshelves, a veritable treasury of aberrant and delinquent behavior. He noticed a tiny totem doll on the shelf, picked it up, and turned it over in his hand.

"Still play with dolls, Doctor?"

Chase didn't look up. "She's a Malaysian dream warden. She stands sentry while you sleep and calms your dreams. Need one?"

"Me? No," Bruce denied quickly. Too quickly. "Only things that need calming in my dreams are the Rockettes."

Chase glanced up and held his gaze. "This letter writer," she announced, "is a total wacko."

"Wacko? That a technical term?"

Chase didn't smile. "The patient apparently suffers from obsessional syndrome with potential homicidal styles."

Bruce tried again. "So what you're saying — this guy's a total wacko, right?"

The slightest of smiles broke the corners of her mouth.

For the first time, Bruce noticed the Batman research stacked in one corner of her desk. Above it, a framed print hung on the wall. A bat. He was curious. "You have a thing for bats?"

Chase followed his gaze. "That's a Rorschach blot, Mr. Wayne. People see what they want to."

Bruce's eyes jerked back to the print. It *was* just an inkblot! Only *he* saw a bat within its bleeding lines.

"I think the question would be" — Chase turned it neatly on him — "do *you* have a thing for bats?"

Bruce changed the subject so abruptly he felt guilty. "So . . . this Riddler — he's dangerous?"

Chase didn't answer directly. "What do you know about obsession?"

Bruce shrugged. "Not much."

"Obsession is born of fear. Recall a moment of great terror in your life. Say you associate that moment with —" She broke off, plucked an image at random. "— a bat. The bat's image becomes a cancer of the mind, grows more real than your daily life. Can you imagine something like that?" She looked directly into his eyes again. "The letter writer is obsessed with you. His only escape may be —"

"— to kill me!" Bruce finished for her.

Chase was impressed by his shrewdness. "You understand obsession better than you let on."

Bruce suddenly looked at his watch. "Oops. Time I was going. I'd love to keep chatting, but I'm going to have to get you out of those clothes."

Chase looked mildly shocked. "Excuse me?"

"And into a black dress," Bruce explained. When she looked mystified, he threw her his best charm-school smile.

"Tell me, Doctor — do you like the circus?"

Despite herself, Chase Meridian smiled back.

Chapter 5

Gotham Circus was a twice-yearly fixture, held in the old Hippodrome by the harbor. On special occasions like tonight's charity benefit, attended by the mayor himself and the Gotham glitterati, it brought capacity crowds flocking to the big-top tent.

They oohed and aahed and gulped and cheered as, seventy feet above the ring, the Flying Graysons soared into their trapeze act. Mother and Father looked impossibly young and athletic, not much older than their two teenage sons, all dressed in colorful red and green spangles.

They swooped and soared and somersaulted as if born to the air, and the crowd went wild.

"Ladies and gentlemen!" The red-coated ringmaster's bullhorn cut over the hubbub. "Tonight's charity benefit has raised almost four hundred thousand dollars for Gotham Children's Hospital." He gestured into the darkness of the audience. "Let's thank our largest single donor: Bruce Wayne!"

A spotlight danced across the crowd, settling on Bruce and Chase in their evening finery. She was embarrassed, but he grinned self-assuredly at the loud applause they garnered.

"And now," the ringmaster went on dramatically, "Richard, the youngest Flying Grayson, will perform the awe-inspiring Death Drop!"

The handsome boy in his mid-teens strode out onto the highest platform, the crowd a single mass far below. He grabbed the trapeze bar and, with a confidence that belied his youth, swung out in an arc above the crowd.

"Fly, Robin, fly," Mr. Grayson whispered.

As he soared over the exact center of the arena, Dick released his grip. He fell, somersaulting, oblivious to the crowd's terrified gasp, his mind focused entirely on the task at hand. Two — three — four times he spun, and just as it seemed certain he would plunge to the sawdust below, there was a blur as his father swung out on a trapeze of his own. Passing Dick at the nadir of his swing, he reached his hand out to grab that of his son.

Swinging on, he kept his grip, hauling Dick after him. Both landed gracefully on the opposite platform.

The ringmaster smiled at the deafening applause. He'd let them take an extra bow tonight. Suddenly something caught his eye. A gloved hand extended through the curtain that separated the ring from the "backstage" area. It beckoned him with a single finger. Puzzled, the ringmaster stepped out of the ring.

In the audience, Bruce's date with Chase was going better than he'd dared hope. "I'm rock climbing Sunday," he told her. "How about coming along?"

Chase sighed. "I'd love to, actually. I love climbing."

Her voice tailed away, and Bruce prompted her: "But —"

" I . . . guess I've met someone."

"Fast work!" Bruce knew he was being unfair, but he couldn't stop himself. "You just moved here!"

Chase looked uncomfortable. "You could say he kind of dropped out of the sky, and bang — I think he felt it, too."

"He sure did," Bruce muttered, only half under his breath.

"What?"

Bruce looked awkward. "I said, who wouldn't?"

He glanced away, toward the center ring, where a tiny car with horns honking was roaring around, dislodging clowns who tumbled and fell over each other. As the Graysons descended from their lofty heights, moving swiftly down the guywires, the ringmaster stepped back into the ring.

" 'A land of light and shadow,' " Chase quoted, " 'where beasts dance and freaks are king.' "

Bruce whirled to face her. "What?"

"It's a description of the circus. From a fairy tale my mother used to —"

Almost exactly what Two-Face had said on the videotape! Bruce grabbed her hand. "We've got to get out of here!"

But the ringmaster was speaking again: "Ladies and gentlemen — your attention, please! Tonight, a new act for your amusement. We call it — Massacre Under the Big Top!"

The man turned, and Bruce caught a glimpse under an arc light. It was Two-Face!

The clowns ripped off their costumes to reveal their true thuggish identities, pulling out machine guns and menacing the panicked crowd. A woman screamed, then another. Children cried.

"People! People!" Two-Face spoke into his mike. "Show some grace under pressure. A little decorum, please." Then, when he saw he was getting no reaction: "Shut up or die!" he bawled.

His gunmen moved into sentry positions at each section of bleachers, their guns covering the crowd, quieter now, though there was plenty of muffled sobbing.

Two of the thugs rolled a round bomb into the ring, attaching the sphere to ropes hanging from the rafters high above. "Inside that orb," Two-Face announced, "two hundred sticks of TNT." He held up a small electronic box. "In our hand, a radio detonator."

He pressed a button, and on the box's digital display a countdown started as the bomb was hoisted up. 2:00 . . . 1:59 . . . 1:58 . . .

"You have two minutes," he told the crowd.

The mayor stood up in his seat. "What do you want?" he blustered, trying to hide his fear, yet feeling it was his duty to be spokesman.

Two-Face considered. "Want, Mr. Mayor? Just one little thing. Batman. Bruised. Broken. Bleeding. In a word: dead."

He turned the handsome side of his face to the fore. "Who do we have assembled here before us? Gotham's finest. Rich. Influential. Smart. One of you must know who Batman is. We'd lay odds one of you *is* Batman!"

Bruce watched, helpless to act, his eyes riveted on the bomb as it rose ever upward.

In the ring, Two-Face spun round, showing off the twisted scars of his evil side. "So, unless the Bat is surrendered to us post haste, we're off on a proverbial killing spree. Citywide mayhem and murder. Starting tonight. With all you lovely folks as our very first corpses. You have two — well, considerably under two — minutes!"

Bruce felt a dryness in his mouth, a sickness in the pit of his being. He had no choice. No secret in this world was worth the price of innocent lives. His decision made, he got to his feet. Chase, misunderstanding, grabbed his arm and tried to pull him back down again. He cleared his throat, ready to confess to the world who he was —

When suddenly several people in the crowd shouted out. People were on their feet, pointing up, screaming.

No one had noticed the Flying Graysons climb stealthily back up their guylines, and now, up in the rafters, they headed toward the bomb.

"Move, move, move!" Two-Face yelled to his men.

Those gunsels who weren't acting sentry took to the guywires, and began clambering up after the acrobats. "Dick, you go!" Dick's father yelled. "We'll hold them off!"

Dick's mother, father, and older brother, Chris, swung with practiced ease from trapeze to guywire to platform, trying to delay the thugs. Two-Face always went for the best in hirelings, and several were themselves trained gymnasts.

Dick swung from one trapeze to another, bounced off the high wire, grabbed a catwalk, and hoisted himself up. Taking advantage of the distraction, Bruce hopped the rail and pushed through the frightened crowd.

The numbers on Two-Face's timer ran inexorably down. 1:03 . . . 1:02 . . . 1:01 . . .

Above, the Graysons tangled with the first thugs. Mr. Grayson kicked off the man who grabbed his leg, and managed to leap to another trapeze. But his wife wasn't so lucky: Trying to prevent a thug from landing on the uppermost platform, she took a roundhouse punch that sent her toppling off.

The crowd below screamed as she plummeted down

through the air. But she managed to hook one leg over a trapeze bar, wrapped her ankle round a rope, and dangled head down.

Bruce moved fast toward one of the sentries, hearing Two-Face's voice cry out: "Forty-five seconds!"

The men who were grappling with Chris and his father above gave up at once, and started to slide back down their ropes. Mr. Grayson and Chris formed a human chain, the man anchoring the teenager so he could swing out toward his dangling mother.

Ignorant of the excitement below, Dick had reached the bomb itself. Frantically fighting to stay calm, he began to unlash its binding ropes.

As the gang began to pour into the trapdoor that would be their escape route, a couple of thrillseekers fired their guns above the crowd's head. Dick scaled a service ladder, not looking down, shoving against the roof hatch. Even as it gave and he swarmed through, Two-Face continued his crazy countdown: "Fifteen seconds, everybody!"

Chris made his final swing. His mother let go, and sailed gloriously through the air toward him. She and her husband had taught the boys the rudiments of trapeze even before they could walk — a baby's arms being much stronger than its legs — and relief flooded through her now as it looked like that training would pay off.

Bruce tapped the watching thug on the shoulder. "Show's over!" He took him out with a single punch and started to sprint toward Two-Face. And then it happened —

Images flashed across his mind once more. A dark alley. A gun firing twice. Red roses. And over it all, Two-Face's voice seemed to echo mockingly: "You're a killer, too!"

Then another thug stepped out and barred his way.

Two-Face was looking up at the dangling Graysons. He reached into his pocket, pulled out his silver dollar, and flipped it in the air. "Always the same old question," he muttered as the coin spun. "Life . . . or death."

The coin had landed scarred side up. Two-Face drew his gun. The timer read 10 seconds.

Even as Bruce felled the second thug, Dick Grayson was climbing out onto the exterior of the big tent. As Bruce ran at Two-Face, Dick was letting the spherical bomb drop from his fingers. And as a third thug took Bruce square with a flying tackle, the bomb rolled down the steep roof toward the harbor below.

Looking down, Mrs. Grayson screamed as Two-Face raised his gun. The first bullet cut the rope that held them. The second severed it completely.

"Never did like the circus," the monster said callously. He turned and ran for the tunnel as the three innocent people fell forty feet to their deaths.

At the moment their bodies hit the big-top floor, the bomb hit the water. The night was split by a funneling explosion.

Dick had swung himself back inside and down onto the

catwalk. He froze at the rail, a chill like ice running down his spine. Sprawled below were the bodies of the three people he loved most in the world.

"NO!!!" His voice was halfway between a strangled scream and a plaintive gasp.

Standing over them, looking up, was Bruce Wayne, his face a tragic echo of Dick's pain.

Chapter 6

Next afternoon, a police car headed up the long, winding drive to Wayne Manor. A pack on his back, Dick Grayson followed behind it on his motorcycle.

Expecting their arrival, Bruce was already waiting on the wide front steps to meet them. As he and Commissioner Gordon greeted each other, Dick dismounted and, looking slightly awestruck by the sheer size of the mansion, wandered into the house.

"It's good of you to take him in," Gordon acknowledged. "He's been filling out forms all day. He hasn't slept or eaten."

Bruce nodded. He watched thoughtfully for a long moment as Gordon and his driver got back into their cruiser, then he followed Dick inside.

In the manor hall, Alfred was already introducing himself to the teenager. "Welcome, Master Grayson. I'm Alfred."

"How ya doin', Al?" the boy replied.

"Al?" the butler echoed, horrified.

"We prepared a room for you upstairs," Bruce said, as he joined them. "Maybe you'd like to eat something first?"

But Dick wasn't listening. He stared over Bruce's shoulder, watching the police cruiser finally disappear down the drive. "Okay," he said, businesslike. "I'm outta here!" He saw Bruce's puzzled frown, and went on: "I figured telling that cop I'd stay here saved me a truckload of social service interviews and goodwill. So no offense, but thanks. See ya!"

As Dick headed for the door, Bruce made a silent signal to Alfred, then hurried out after the boy.

"Where will you go?" Bruce asked. "The circus is halfway to Metropolis by now."

Dick's mouth was set in a hard, grim line. "I'm going to get a fix on Two-Face. Then I'm going to kill him!"

"Killing him won't take the pain away," Bruce said gently. "It'll make it worse."

"Spare me the sermons!" Dick said emotionally. "I don't need your advice. Or your charity."

Dick was getting heated, looking for any excuse to let out the pain and anger and grief that welled inside him.

Bruce had to cool things down. "Nice bike," he remarked, running his eye over Dick's machine. It was in good condition, showed several signs that someone put a lot of time and care into looking after it. But the boy wasn't buying.

"You a big motorcycle fan, Bruce?" he said skeptically. "Hang out at a lot of biker bars?"

"I know a little about bikes," Bruce replied simply. He watched as Dick mounted his hog, and noticed that the gas gauge was reading empty. "Well, good luck." He shrugged, as if accepting the inevitable. "Oh, you might want to fill up in our garage. No gas stations for miles."

The Wayne garage was larger than most people's houses. Five vintage automobiles were stored there, including a Rolls-Royce, a Bentley, and an Alfa Romeo Spyder.

Dick's eyes lit up. "Oh man!" he breathed.

"Pump's this way." Bruce led him past the cars, and Dick's eyes grew even wider as he saw the other collection — the vintage motorbikes. He stared in awe.

"That's a BMW 950. A Kawasaki Razor. And that's a Harley Mongoose!" Dick shook his head, impressed. "I think they only made ten."

"Seven, actually," Bruce corrected him. "She's our pride and joy. Doesn't run, though."

Dick considered. "Probably the gearbox," he diagnosed. "They were touchy. And sometimes the fuel caps carbonized."

"I've been looking for someone to restore them," Bruce told him, truthfully. "Whoever did it — if he actually got them going — could take any bike he wanted as a fee. Plus room and board while he worked on them." He paused for the briefest of moments. "Too bad you're not staying around. Anyway, have a good trip."

As if his entrance had been timed — which it had, almost — Alfred appeared with a tray of appetizing food. Rare London broil, with baby potatoes and fresh greens. "Oh, is the young master leaving? Pity. I'll just toss this away, then. Perhaps the dogs are hungry."

Alfred turned back into the house. Dick stared after him hungrily. He looked at the bikes, then made his decision.

"Maybe just a couple of days," he said to Bruce. "'Til I get these babies purring." Bruce smiled to himself as Dick grabbed his knapsack and hurried after the butler, calling: "Yo, Al! Hold up!"

It would be good to have someone else around this lonely old house.

Two gunshots split the night. Two coffins. His parents.

Mourners fill the house. Thunder cracks outside, and a young Bruce Wayne sees a leather-bound book on the desk.

Suddenly, the storm's wildest gust. The front door flies open, and an evil wind whips the book's pages.

The window explodes, shattering glass, and out of the darkness flies a huge, evil bat.

"Master Bruce?" Alfred's voice cut through his reverie, and it took him a moment to gather his thoughts.

He was sitting in a chair in the old-fashioned library, lights out even though it was dark outside, a framed photo of his parents and himself as a boy on the table beside him. A single red rose was held loosely in his hand, taken from the vase on the shelf.

"Just like my parents," Bruce said, and Alfred noticed that his eyes were red. "It's happening again. A monster comes out of the night. A scream. Two gunshots. I killed them."

"What did you say?" Alfred queried, his voice sharp.

"He killed them," Bruce went on. "Two-Face. He slaughtered Dick's family."

"No," Alfred said firmly. "You said 'I' — '*I* killed them.'"

Suddenly the darkness outside was broken by a beam of light. The Bat-Signal. Gordon needed him.

The conversation was at an end. Bruce hurried from the room, speaking over his shoulder. "Take care of the kid."

Upstairs, in the guest bedroom he'd selected, Dick Grayson stood staring blindly out the window. He wanted to cry, to rage, to rant and roar . . . but everything inside him just felt numb.

There was a soft knock, and Alfred entered. "Can I help you settle in, young sir?"

"No," Dick said gruffly, then added: "Thanks. I won't be here long."

Alfred picked up the motorcycle helmet that lay on the bed, and saw the stylized bird figure that was painted on it. "A robin?"

Dick didn't feel like explaining, but he did anyway. "My brother's wire broke during a show. I swung out, caught him. Afterward my dad called me his hero, said I flew like a robin." His voice caught in his throat. "Some hero I turned out to be!"

"Ah, but your father was right," Alfred said comfortingly. "You are a hero. I can tell. Broken wings mend in time. Perhaps one day Robin will fly again."

As Alfred left, Dick pulled open his knapsack. Several newspaper clippings spilled out, all items concerning Two-Face.

The boy sat and stared at them with mounting obsession.

The Batmobile safely parked in a shadowed alley, Batman swung up into the rooftops on his line. The giant spotlight that cast the signal stood on the flat roof of Police HQ — but as Batman leaped down from a neighboring roof, he saw that it was unattended.

"Commissioner Gordon?"

A shadow moved from behind the searchlight. He was surprised to see Chase Meridian standing there.

"Gordon's gone home," she informed him. "I sent the signal."

"Why? What's wrong?"

Chase spoke quickly: "I was at the circus last night — with Bruce Wayne. I noticed something about Two-Face. His coin. He's obsessed with justice. It's his Achilles' heel. It can be exploited."

"You called me here for that?" Grim, intimidating, Batman took a step closer to her, looming over her like some night-beast. "The Bat-Signal is not a beeper!"

He'd expected her to back off, but again Chase surprised him. She moved even closer. "I wish I could say my interest in you was purely professional."

He stood very still. Her hand reached up, and she ran her fingers along the outline of Batman's mask. He knew she was as attracted to him as he was to her, but now was surely not the right time. He moved his own hand to stop hers.

"I'm not the kind of guy who blends in at a family picnic," he said.

Chase smiled. "We could give it a try. I'll bring the food, you bring your scarred psyche."

He couldn't help admiring her. "You're direct, aren't you?"

"You like strong women. I've done my homework." Chase smiled again. "Or do I need skintight vinyl and a whip?"

She was referring to the Catwoman, of course. "I haven't had much luck with women," he said, a little rueful.

"Maybe you just haven't met the right woman."

They were so close she could have stretched up and kissed him without any trouble. But the moment was broken as Commissioner Gordon, trench coat hastily flung over his pajamas, came rushing onto the roof.

"I saw the beacon," he gasped. "What's going on?"

"Nothing." Batman turned away. "It was a false alarm."

Chase and Gordon stood watching as he dived from the building, swung down, and leaped into the Batmobile.

"Are you sure?" she said to herself, so softly that Gordon didn't even know she'd spoken.

Chapter 7

Batman was unhappy as the Batmobile sped away from the alley. Normally he didn't mix business and pleasure; the night was for fighting crime, not for playing lovey-dovey with some woman . . . no matter how beautiful she was. But he had to admit to himself: Chase Meridian had really gotten under his skin.

The sleek machine raced up an on-ramp and joined Gotham's elevated roadway system, snaking between buildings, powering alongside aqueduct archways so large they might have been built for giants.

Behind one of the arches, an armored car lay in wait. At the controls — Two-Face. As the Batmobile sped by unheeding, the master criminal spoke into a microphone. "Gentlemen, start your engines."

Almost instantly, two red-and-black cars — bisected

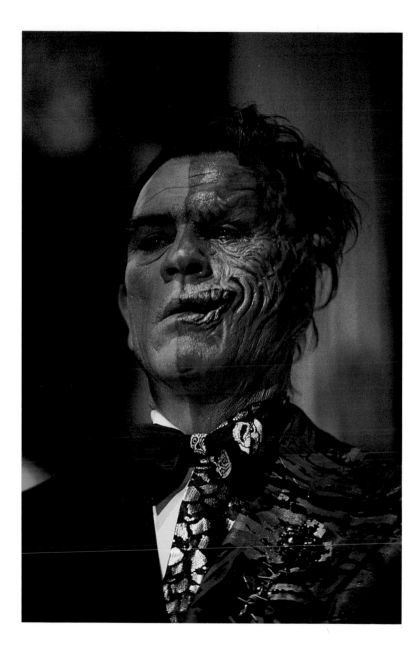

down the middle, just like Two-Face himself — came racing out of their hiding place, closing fast on the Batmobile.

As Batman caught their lights behind him, he snapped: "Tactical!" The voice-activated graphics leaped into life on the Batmobile's console screen, another two winking dots joining the first pair as more of Two-Face's pursuit cars raced across the elevated roadway to join the chase. A fifth — Two-Face's own car — took up the rear.

Never one to merely react if it was at all possible to change the odds against him, Batman sent the 'mobile barreling off the aqueducts and onto the actual rooftops, searing away from the pursuit cars across tarpaper flats. The lead pursuit car fell into line behind him, machine guns set into the two-toned hood spitting bullets that ricocheted off the Batmobile's armored sides.

Dead ahead, an abyss between two roofs yawned. Batman's foot stabbed the accelerator and the car's twin turbos roared into life, carrying it over the chasm below. Front wheels grabbed the opposite roof, spinning and screaming for purchase. Then he was over, and aware that the first of Two-Face's men was also trying the jump.

The red-and-black car soared — but not high enough. It fell short, its trajectory carrying it into the wall of the opposite building, where it exploded in fiery violence.

The second pursuit vehicle banked off the side of an apartment complex, bounced its way down several adjacent roofs, and screeched into line mere feet behind the

Batmobile. Batman switched direction abruptly, steering toward a narrow drop. On the other side was the sloping roof of the Gotham Insurance Company, rising like a steep hill.

Again the Batmobile took off, leaped through space, and hit the roof. Immediately, tiny suction cups protruded from the tires, adhering to the steep surface.

Seeing the Batmobile roar off up the manmade hill, the thug behind thought he could do it, too. He made the jump all right — but unfortunately, there were no suction cups in his tires. His wheels spun in vain for grip, screeching and smoking. Then the car slid slowly backward off the building, tumbling down to crash in a vacant lot far below.

On Batman's screen, a second light winked out. Then the others gunned their cars to close in on him, Two-Face still bringing up the rear.

The Batmobile shot down a narrow alley of rooftops, sheer skyscraper walls rising on both sides. Dead ahead — a giant building, a massive mural painted on its side.

"Cook him!" Two-Face rasped into his mike. On his gunsels' cars, cannons unfolded from the hoods. One fired, and a tremendous fireball exploded close behind the Batmobile. A second shot exploded overhead.

Strapped into his seat, Batman saw the mural racing toward him through the windshield. He hit a button on the dashboard, and sophisticated circuitry sprang into action. A tiny hood-hatch was blown out, shooting a Bat-grapple high into the air. It caught on the wings of a giant stone gargoyle, one of many that stood sentinel atop the building.

A small but potent winch activated, jerking the Bat-grapple cable tight. The mighty machine was yanked vertical, and Batman rode straight up the side of the building, the painted mural flashing beneath his wheels.

Neither of the pursuit cars could stop in time, twin explosions marking their destruction as they slammed at high speed into the mural wall. Above, the Batmobile braked to a halt on the roof, turned, and took off again across the elevated cityscape.

Two-Face cursed as his own car came to a skidding halt barely inches away from the mural. He stepped out, lit by the flickering flames of the two wrecks, and screamed his rage into the night.

Two-Face's hideout was in a place few people knew of and fewer still had seen. In the bowels of an ancient support arch of the Gotham Bridge, a giant face had been carved in relief in the stone. Behind it, a chamber that once had been used to store equipment was now a palace fit for the two-edged villain's obsession.

Two-Face had returned alone from the latest attempt on Batman's life, and was pacing the room in frustration.

"The Bat's stubborn refusal to expire is driving us insane!" he growled.

Sugar and Spice, his two female lieutenants, knew when to keep quiet. It didn't pay to upset the boss when he was like this. They sat silently, trying to ignore him, each watching her own small TV with the sound turned down.

"Then you need help."

The voice spoke from the shadows at the far corner of the room, and Two-Face reacted as soon as he heard it. Twin pistols leaped into his hand, and he swiveled to point them at the mysterious figure standing in the dark.

"Easy," the voice said. "I'm a friend. You can call me —" The figure stepped out into the light. He wore an emerald mask over his eyes, wore an old-fashioned derby hat, and carried a cane. The emerald-green costume that encased his body was covered with question marks. "— the Riddler!"

Two-Face angrily grabbed the newcomer and pushed him hard against the wall. "We'll call you dead, more like! How did you find us? Talk!"

The Riddler grinned, maddeningly. "I think not, my twinned pals. For then what would keep you from slaying me?"

"You got sixty seconds. After that, you'll beg for bullets!"

"Has anyone ever told you you have a serious impulse-control problem? All right, I'll talk."

The Riddler tried to slither free, his awkward body accentuated by the tight, figure-hugging costume. But Two-Face jammed a gun barrel up each nostril and snarled: "Show's over. Let's see if you bleed green."

The Riddler shrugged. "Go ahead. Fire away. But before you do, one question: Is it really me you want to kill?"

His hands came together, the thumbs knitting. He waved them over an exposed lightbulb. On the wall, the shadow of the Bat appeared. "Do you know about hate, my dual-visaged friend?" Riddler hissed. "Slow, burning hate that keeps you awake in the night? I do."

He moved away, started to circle round Two-Face, his movements theatrical and over the top. "Killing him seems like a good idea. But have you thought it through? A few bullets, a quick spray of blood, and then what? Nothing. Is it really enough?"

Two-Face considered. There was truth in this guy's words. He listened with more interest as Riddler continued: "Why not ruin him first? Expose his frailty. And then, when he is at his weakest . . . crush him in your hand!"

Riddler pressed a stud on his cane, and suddenly Sugar and Spice were transfixed to their televisions by the lurid green glow of the Box. White brain-drain beams shot from each Box into the very center of their foreheads.

Riddler held out his receiver to Two-Face. "This is how I found you. Take a hit and see." He tapped his forehead. "It makes you smarter."

Two-Face hesitated no more than a fraction of a second. He tentatively lifted the receiver to his skull — and was immediately blasted with a dose of Sugar and Spice's neural energy. And Two-Face understood.

"You correlated all dualities in the city — orders of half-and-half pizza, wine splits, two-toned clothing — cross-referenced all addresses with multiples of two, crunched the probabilities by bicoastal, bizonal localities, leading you . . . here." Then, as he realized exactly what this thing was doing to his intelligence levels: "Holy heck!"

Riddler pulled away Two-Face's receiver, but the gang boss reached greedily for it again. "More!" he demanded.

"Only the first one's free," Riddler told him. "Here's the concept: Crime. My IQ, your AK-47. This is the bargain: You will help me gather production capital so I can manufacture enough of these . . ." He paused and pulled out one of his Boxes. "Enough to build an empire that will eclipse Bruce Wayne's forever. In return, I will help you solve the greatest riddle of them all. Who is Batman? Then we'll find him and kill him."

Two-Face eyed his would-be ally and pulled his coin from his pocket. He never, ever made any decision of this magnitude without consulting the coin. "Heads, we take your offer." He rested the barrel of his gun on the Riddler's temple. "Tails, we blow your riddling head off!"

Under the mask, Edward Nygma sweated. This wasn't supposed to happen! He'd forgotten to take Two-Face's madness into account. He cursed bitterly to himself. All the potential that was going to be released by his new costume . . . his new identity . . . his new business venture — and it depended on the toss of a coin.

He watched in silent prayer as it flipped over and over in the air.

Chapter 8

The palette of black jeweler's felt was littered with bright, sparkling diamonds. The Riddler dropped a piece of paper with his latest riddle on it; he was going to make riddles his trademark, he'd decided. He slipped on a monocle, reached down to pick up a stone, and appraised it admiringly. Two-Face was less patient; he swept the whole lot up into a sack and headed for another counter.

Two-Face's silver coin had come down heads, and the new partners were celebrating in the way they knew best: by breaking the law. Gaining entry to the Gotham Jewelry Exchange, guarded by heavy electronic security during nighttime hours, hadn't been easy. But both villains' minds had been expanded to the point where it had been a puzzle of a few moments' duration to figure out the

number codes and bypass the alarms. And as for the Batman . . .

More than a mile east, the Batmobile cruised the river
highway on Batman's irregular nightly patrol. Connected
to Police Department computers, the car was a veritable
arsenal against crime in its own right.

Now, a flashing message illuminated in the windshield's head-up display. "Crime in progress."

The ever-changing tactical map on the console screen
showed his narrowing proximity to the crime site.

He braked to a halt in the street as the marker indicated
he'd reached his goal. He leaped out and smashed through
the door that barred his way —

To be greeted by a chorus of shrieks and laughter as he
found himself standing in a late-night beauty salon.

Ignoring the girls' teasing banter, Batman left. Beneath
the mask he was fuming. He'd been misled. But how?

Bruce Wayne watched the news as he dressed in suit
and tie next morning. Over a graphic of the riddle left at
the jewelry exchange, the newsreader narrated the story:
"— millions in diamonds stolen, with no sign of Batman.
Teamed with Two-Face is a new criminal, whose pattern
of marking his crimes with puzzles has Gothamites calling him the Riddler."

Bruce pursed his lips. He'd known that scrambling the Batcomputer's downlinks to misdirect him to that salon was too sophisticated for Two-Face. So he had a partner!

The screen caught his interest again as a shot of Edward Nygma came into focus. He was standing on Claw Island, a small island in Gotham Harbor that had long been abandoned.

"In other news," the reader's flat tones went on, "entrepreneur Edward Nygma has signed a lease for Claw Island. Nygma says he plans to break ground on an electronics plant . . ."

Competition! Bruce thought wryly. He flicked off the set, and left the room.

Down in the garage, Dick Grayson had been at work for an hour already. Now he was taking time off, working out in the garage gym, pounding away at one of the straw-filled dummies he'd found there. With every blow he struck home, the teenager thought of Two-Face.

An engine revved, and Dick pivoted to face Bruce, who was straddling the Black Knight motorbike, his eyes dancing.

"She sounds great. You've done a good job," he told the boy. "Why don't you grab the Harley and we'll take a ride?"

Dick seemed reluctant, almost sullen. "Look, man," he

said, "I appreciate the gig, but let's leave it at that. We're not gonna be buddies. You don't even know me."

Bruce's eyes lost their twinkle, hardened as he thought of his own bitter past. "I know the pain's with you every day," he replied. "The shame. Feeling that somehow you should have saved them." He knew those feelings all too well; he'd known them for way too many years now. "You're right, Dick," he went on. "I don't know you. But I'm like you." He paused a second, then: "The Wayne Foundation has an excellent scholarship fund. Have you thought about your future?"

For an answer, Dick thrust out a copy of the *Gotham Times*. Front-page news, with picture, was Two-Face. "He's my future!"

"Don't let your love, your passion for your family, twist into hatred of Two-Face," Bruce counseled. "It's too easy."

Angrily, Dick grabbed his benefactor by the shirtfront. "No offense, man — but I don't think you've a lot to teach me!"

"Don't be too sure," Bruce said quietly.

Dick released his hold, started away, then stared in disbelief as Bruce threw roundhouse punches — one, two, three — with staccato precision at the dummy's head. He moved so fast, it was almost like one continuous blow.

Dick could only stare and wonder.

The outrageous robberies continued, each night at a different venue. Gotham Casino. Virginia Towers luxury apartment development. The Dirk Maggs Radio Center. O'Neil's Exclusive Restaurant. Each time, Batman found himself in a different location entirely. And he didn't have clue one as to how they were doing it.

Of course, he kept up his running battle with the city's other criminals — scarcely a night went by without his stopping muggers, heist-men, or thieves.

But Two-Face and Riddler began to occupy almost all his thoughts, and catching them was his number-one priority.

And while crime haunted his waking moments, the dream haunted his sleep.

Always the same — the gunshots, the wake, the leather book. Running, running into the storm-filled night.

Why? What had frightened him so much?

Out on Claw Island, a truly herculean construction neared completion, surreptitiously using the laundered profits from the deadly duo's string of crimes. Developed from the Riddler's own detailed plans and designs, the factory that arose on the derelict little chunk of rock was to be entirely automated.

Edward Nygma was the darling of the media. But he refused to say exactly what it was his revolutionary new factory would be making. It was to be a surprise . . . and then some. If they had only known!

Bruce's relationship with Chase Meridian continued to develop, although he was never really sure how she felt about him. Oh, he knew how she felt about the Batman all right — she'd as good as told him. But she seemed to prefer to keep things light when it was just Bruce and her, and it was beginning to get to him.

Of course, the fact that he'd had to cancel several dates in a row because of crises caused by Two-Face and Riddler didn't help matters any. From her apartment in the city, he knew that Chase's window gave a good view of the Bat-Signal when it went up from Police HQ.

He wondered if she ever noticed the coincidence — when the signal was up, he canceled on her. Funny, to think she only cared for half of him. He felt a bit like Two-Face himself.

Came Edward's great day, and the new corporation — Nygmatech — started production.

Dressed like Bruce Wayne down to the smallest detail, Edward held court with the city's media. "Now all can be revealed," he told them proudly, holding up the first commercial models of his patented Box. "Nygmatech brings the joy of three-dimensional, holographic entertainment into every home! I have seen the future, ladies and gentlemen of the press . . . and the future is me!"

"Ahem!"

Alfred's discreet cough took Dick by surprise. Flushing a little with embarrassment, he guiltily stepped away from the door he'd been trying to open.

"May I help you, Master Richard?" the butler asked.

Dick jerked his thumb toward the door. "How come this is the only locked door in this museum? What's back there?"

"Master Wayne's dead wives," Alfred told him drily. He had a wry smile on his lips as he watched the boy go. He waited until the coast was absolutely clear, then disappeared into the secret doorway that led down to the Batcave.

Hidden in an alcove, his eyes drinking in every detail, Dick Grayson nodded to himself. He'd soon find out!

The Nygmatech Box was a soaraway success, priced precisely where it would generate maximum profit while also gaining maximum sales. Two-Face and Riddler could have become millionaires by running it as a legitimate business.

But decency and honesty had no part in their plans.

Electronic outlets throughout the city reported sellouts on the first day, and the Claw Island factory was put into round-the-clock production. Rich men bought one for every member of their family; poor men bought one to share between everyone, huddled round together to enjoy the show; crooked men shoplifted as many as they could, and did a roaring trade at double price on the black market.

And, had anyone known or cared who he was, Alfred Pennyworth, butler to playboy Bruce Wayne and the Batman, might have been seen to purchase one in an exclusive uptown store.

3-D was the Gotham rage, and nobody could afford to be without the Box.

Chapter 9

On a preset night, at a prearranged time, Edward Nygma — alias the Riddler — hooked his invention into the electronic web formed by the Gotham-wide use of the Box. From a million Boxes, the pulsing white beam leaped at a million foreheads, draining the minds of the people engrossed in their new 3-D televisions.

Beams of shimmering white light issued from the back of each Box, shooting out of windows, through walls, into the night sky. They flowed together, joined with others just the same, until the entire city skyline was covered by a pulsing spiderweb of neural energy . . . all focused on the mysterious building on Claw Island.

In his Master Control Room, Riddler sat atop a tremendous electronic throne. Overhead, a huge diode delivered pulses of glowing neural energy directly to his brain. Rivulets of the stuff pulsed and glowed as they flowed over his skin. His mind raced with a hundred million new facts and figures and feelings.

He sighed. "So this is what it's like to be God!" he said to himself.

Deep in the Batcave, Alfred watched a computer simulation of a screaming bat.

"I see the new sonic modification isn't running yet," he remarked. Bruce looked up from the riddles he was poring over. "I'm confident it will never work."

"You said that about the Batmobile," Bruce shot back, before returning to the riddles, comparative forensic data scrolling up on his screens.

"Same obscure paper stock," he read aloud. "No prints. Definitely the same author. Like — 'The eight of us go forth, not back, to protect our king from a foe's attack.' Pawns."

"I couldn't agree more," Alfred sighed. "We're all just pawns in these madmen's games —"

But Bruce broke in: "No, Alfred. That's the answer to the riddle. Chess pawns. A clock, a match, pawns. All physical objects. Manmade . . ."

"Small in size," Alfred joined in. He and Bruce frequently free-associated like this. Surprising how often the method led to usable clues. "Light in weight."

"Time. Fire. Battle strategy. What's the connection, Alfred?"

"With all due respect, sir," the butler replied, "I think that's why they call him the Riddler!"

Bruce crossed the work area to where the Box Alfred had bought was waiting to be disassembled. Maybe this would give him the answers he needed.

Carefully, not wanting to break whatever was inside, Bruce managed to ease off the protective casing . . . only to see the electronic circuitry inside vaporize in an instant before his eyes.

Some kind of self-destruct, obviously. But why? What corporation in the world would go to that extent to protect an invention on which they could surely take out a patent anyway?

Alfred left the laundry room and moved across the flagstone tiles of the mansion's wide hall. He paused near the secret entrance to the Batcave and called out: "Master Dick?"

High above, Dick appeared on the third-floor landing. "Up here, Al."

"Just checking, young sir."

Dick disappeared again, and Alfred moved on to the door, cautiously opening it. Above, flattened against the wall, Dick prepared to move. *Four seconds,* he thought.

He waited till he heard the click of the opening lock. *From . . . now!*

As Alfred disappeared into the tunnel that led down to the cave, and the door began to close behind him, Dick moved.

Leaping the banister like the athlete he was, he grabbed the chandelier and swung across to a large tapestry. Letting go, he slid down the massive cloth and sprinted for the door.

He dived into the passage and the door slammed shut behind him. Unable to stop himself, Dick rolled through a dark doorway, tumbled down the long stairway that it led to, and landed on the floor of the Batcave.

Alfred turned at the commotion, and the two stared at each other in utter disbelief.

Bruce had finally kept a date with Chase. They'd enjoyed dinner at an exclusive restaurant he knew, and had a wonderful time. Now, she'd invited him back to her apartment for a nightcap and more chat.

"Who's your decorator? U-Haul?" Bruce quipped, seeing the stacks of half-opened boxes and cases, clothes and books strewn everywhere. She'd been so busy working, she'd had little time to settle in.

Chase disappeared into the kitchen to make coffee. She came back with a small box and handed it to him. Inside was one of the small wicker dream dolls. "Call it clinical intuition," Chase said. "I thought your dreams might need changing."

Bruce looked at her long and hard. He thought more of this woman than he had of anyone for a long time. He needed someone to unburden himself to . . . and, as a psychologist, she might even be able to help.

"My parents were murdered," he said, as steadily as he could. "In front of me. I was just a kid."

Chase nodded, silent, waiting for him to go on.

"I can't remember exactly what happened. I get flashes, in my dreams. Most of it makes sense, but there's one element . . . one I don't understand. A book. A leather-bound book."

"There's something else, isn't there?" Chase's voice was little more than a whisper.

"Yes. The dreams have started coming when I'm awake."

There — it was out! He'd had no idea how he would react to sharing this secret and was surprised at the sheer relief he felt.

"You're describing repressed memories," Chase explained. "Images of some forgotten pain trying to surface."

Just then the kettle in the kitchen started to whistle, and Chase hurried off, murmuring that she'd be right back.

Agitated, Bruce paced the room. Passing her desk, he saw it had become a virtual shrine to Batman. Articles, news photos, magazine pieces. He picked up a file marked with Batman's name, and swung round as Chase spoke behind him: "Is it possible there's an aspect of your parents' death you haven't faced? You were so young . . ."

Bruce held up the Batman file. "Why do I feel like the other man here, Doctor?"

"Please, Bruce, don't change the subject!"

But he wouldn't be swayed. He couldn't be. Amazingly, he felt jealous of her interest in his darker half. But it didn't make sense, he tried to tell himself. How could he be jealous of himself?

His voice was cold: "I'd say all this goes beyond taking your work home."

Chase shrugged. "All right. He's fascinating. Clinically fascinating." She touched a button on the console, and news footage of Batman fighting appeared on her monitor screen. "Why does a man do this?"

"Look at the abuse he's taking," Bruce pointed out. "He's not just fighting crime."

"It's as if he's paying some great penance." Chase looked thoughtful, stroking her chin. "What crime could he have committed to deserve a life of nightly torture?"

Bruce didn't like the way this conversation was going. He felt uncomfortable at the thought of where it might lead. He leaned forward abruptly, hit a key, and the screen went blank. "So . . . Batman had a lousy childhood. That it, Doc?"

Chase grabbed his hand as it came away from the

keyboard. "Why do you throw up that superficial mask?" she demanded. "I want to be close, but you won't let me near. What are you protecting me from?"

He didn't know what to say, but it didn't matter anyway. Before he could figure an appropriate reply, the beeper on his wristwatch started to sound. Bruce voice-activated it, and Chase stared in surprise as the face turned into a tiny screen with an image of Alfred on it. Another of WayneTech's expensive, and extremely hard to come by, gadgets.

"Sorry to bother you, sir." The digitalized voice was flat, inflected in all the wrong places, but still recognizable as Alfred's. "I have some rather distressing news about Master Richard. I'm afraid he has gone traveling."

Bruce frowned. "He ran away?"

"He took the car, sir."

"He boosted the Jaguar?" Bruce was relieved. "Is that all?"

"The other car, sir," Alfred said patiently. He knew where Bruce was, and had to be discreet.

"The Bentley?"

"No, sir. The *other* other car."

Bruce closed his eyes and gave an audible groan as he realized precisely what the butler meant. The Batmobile!

Dick had taken the Batmobile!

Chapter 10

Arkham Square, with its trashy neon bars, was the very center of everything that was bad about Gotham. Even though it was getting late, street life was barely beginning. The hustlers were out in force, whispering deals to the tourists, eyes open, ever ready for an opportunist scam. Slow-moving cars cruised by, their occupants looking for booze or drugs or just plain trouble.

Deek Mowgli and his gang of three teenagers had drunk too much, and now they were ready for action. A man in a pinstripe suit, briefcase in hand, weaved an unsteady route across the square. A businessman, tipsy after an office party, perhaps. It didn't matter — he meant cash, and credit cards. The gang followed him with their eyes, hungrily, waiting until he was just about to pass them before making their play.

Then Deek signaled, and they moved as if one, surrounding the confused man, barging into him, bustling him into the mouth of the alleyway where they'd been waiting. Deek's hand clasped over the man's mouth, and then —

The roar of a supercharged engine. Heads turned as a sleek, jet-black roadster powered into the square, pulling up at the crosswalk near the alley.

"Chill, dudes," Deek cautioned. "It's the Batman!"

They watched as the car's windshield wipers leaped into life. Then the Bat-foil opened and closed several times before the car's hydraulics engaged and it shot up and down on its springs like a clown's car at the circus. The cockpit opened, then immediately snapped shut again. Whoever was in there didn't know how to operate the controls!

"It ain't the Bat!" Deek spat.

Suddenly the businessman came to his senses and realized what was happening. He gave a strangled yell and broke away, lashing out with his case. He ran blindly up the alley, the gang in close pursuit.

The Batmobile slammed into gear and tore after them, screeching to a halt with the gang silhouetted in the glare of its headlamps. They'd caught up with the man again, who whimpered as they menaced him.

"Who the devil are you?" Deek demanded, as Dick Grayson stepped from the vehicle's hatch.

"I'm the Batman," Dick said, in a low, ominous voice.

He looked down, as if surprised to see the casual T-shirt and jeans he wore. "Did I forget to dress again?"

Deek snapped his fingers, and his gang moved into action once more. One rushed at Dick, a second whirled a heavy length of chain over his head. Dick's hand shot out, grabbing the chain. He open-palmed the thug in the chin, whipping the chain so it took the first man hard in the gut.

"The Caped Crusader strikes again," Dick said lightly. "Without cape, of course."

A third thug charged at him, but Dick leaped high with a flying front kick, knocking him flat on his back. "Another victory for the Dark Knight."

Deek was the only one left on his feet, the other three gang members groaning and writhing on the pavement in pain. His jaw dropped as Dick smiled at him.

"Is your will up to date?"

Deek didn't wait. He took to his heels and ran.

Dick felt pleased with himself. *Not bad,* he thought. *I could definitely get behind this super hero gig!*

The businessman grabbed his hand and shook it frantically as he gasped out his gratitude. Dick shrugged, about to make light of things, when Deek suddenly reappeared. He hadn't gone far — merely to a local bar where guys like him hung out. Now he was back, and Dick's heart sank as he saw the assortment of at least two dozen men who faced him.

"Run," he told the businessman, then with a lot more conviction than he felt, he said: "I'll hold them off."

He knew as he faced them that he didn't have a chance. He was a fine acrobat, and he'd practiced martial arts for as long as he could remember, but he knew his limits. There were just too many of them. Dick flexed his ankles, ready to leap for the nearest fire escape — but a glance upward revealed that they'd closed off that escape route. They were waiting on the roof, too.

Oh well, he thought, only one thing to do! He ran straight at the throng of thugs, jumped high in the air, and right onto the shoulders of the leading man. He kicked off at once, onto the next man, and the next, surefootedly keeping his balance as he weaved from shoulder to head to shoulder again. Just a few more and he'd be at the Bat-mobile —

Then a hand reached up, managed to grab his ankle, and hauled him down into the mass of wrongdoers. Dick struck out wildly as fists and boots thudded into him, but he knew he didn't have a hope.

No one saw the shadow as it fell across them. No one heard the dark figure as it dropped from the rooftops. No one even knew of the Batman's presence until he was suddenly among them, his feet and hands a blur as he dealt out pain and unconsciousness to Dick's attackers.

Almost a dozen fell in the onslaught before the others saw sense and took off up the alley.

Batman turned to Dick, anxious that he be all right — but the teenager's eyes were blazing with fury.

"You!" he yelled, his pointing finger accusing the man who'd opened his house to him and taken him in. "You killed my family!" He swung a punch at Batman's jaw, which was easily avoided, then kicked out at his chest. Batman jumped back to escape it. "If you'd let Two-Face see who you were that night at the circus, they'd still be alive!"

Stepping closer to Batman, Dick hammered on his chest with both hands clenched. Batman held his ground, waiting till the boy's rage was spent and his blows slowed and finally stopped.

"It's all your fault." His voice was broken, pathetic, like a child's . . . and then, finally, in the outpouring of grief he'd tried so hard to deny, Dick broke down and cried.

Later that night, in the Batcave, Bruce tried to explain.

"I tried to tell Two-Face who I was. But Chase pulled me down. Everything happened so fast . . ." His voice trailed away. "Dick, I wish there was something I could do to change things."

"There is." Something had been growing inside Dick ever since he'd found out Bruce Wayne was the Batman. Now, it burst from him in a way even he never expected: "Let me be a part of this!"

Bruce listened as his charge went on: "It's all I think about. Getting Two-Face. He took everything . . . my whole life. But when I was out there tonight — in that alley — I imagined it was him I was fighting. And all the hurt went away. Do you understand that?"

"Only too well."

"So how do we find him?" Dick rushed on. "And when we do, you gotta let me be the one to kill him!"

"Killing damns you." Bruce's tone said that he knew what he was talking about. "It makes you as bad as the criminals you go after. Batman has never killed, and he never will. All this . . . it isn't about revenge."

Dick glanced at the framed newspaper front page with the photo of the Waynes and the announcement that they'd been shot dead by an unknown mugger. He knew that Bruce lived with exactly the same pain that he did.

"Somewhere along the way," the older man was saying, "it stops being a choice, and becomes an addiction. You fight night after night, trying to fill the emptiness. But the pain is always back in the morning."

"Save the speeches about how great you want my life to be, Bruce," Dick said coldly. "You want to help me? Train me. Let me be your partner."

"No."

Dick looked him straight in the eyes. "I *will* be part of this, Bruce. Whether you want me to or not."

Suddenly, Bruce Wayne felt very tired.

NYGMATECH, the banner draped across the front of the prestigious Ritz Hotel proclaimed in three-foot-high letters. IMAGINE THE FUTURE!

Limousines pulled up in twos and threes, disgorging their designer-dressed passengers — Gotham's rich and famous. All were gathering here tonight, invited to the launch of the latest version of Edward Nygma's astounding 3-D Television Box.

Alfred Pennyworth expertly swung the Bentley into a parking slot, and held open the rear doors as Bruce, Dick, and Chase Meridian got out. Chase clinging to Bruce's arm, they made their way into the party inside.

The room was packed with the high and mighty sipping cocktails, nibbling delicately on hors d'oeuvres. The loud buzz of half a hundred different conversations made it sound like the interior of some massive beehive.

Music cut across the chatter as a band struck up, and a few couples took to the dance floor.

Throughout the room, brightly lit stations bore signs announcing The New Box. Pretty showgirls smilingly invited partygoers to step behind the black drapes that lined the booths for the experience of a lifetime. Monitors outside each booth showed the action within — eager participants enjoying total holographic environments created by this revised version of Nygma's Box. Among the many benefits it boasted was full audience interaction.

Bruce scanned the room as he and Chase paused by the

first display. A giggling socialite passed them and stepped inside. Seconds later, the monitor showed her gasping with delight, apparently covered from head to toe in a billion dollars' worth of sparkling diamonds.

The next screen showed a chubby man, sword in hand, battling furiously against a tough-looking knight on horseback.

Everywhere there were little cries of surprise and pleasure, as people made their dreams come true — at least in a three-dimensional hologram. As soon as the Box was switched off they returned to their mundane reality.

The scene seemed to amuse Chase, but Bruce glowered suspiciously. Fully interactive holography, obviously. There must be an electroneural link with the viewer's brain. But if Nygma could introduce images *into* the mind, what was to keep him from drawing images *out?*

Dick left them in pursuit of a pretty showgirl, and they were alone for the first time. "About last night," Bruce began. "I want you to know —"

"It's important to me we stay friends," Chase interrupted.

"Yeah. Definitely. Me, too."

If Chase recognized the sarcasm in his voice, she didn't show it. "Then it's settled. Friends."

But as they broke eye contact, neither looked happy.

Then Edward Nygma made his entrance. Dressed in vintage Bruce Wayne style, even his hair an exact copy of

Bruce's, he gestured theatrically to the host of journalists who flanked him.

"You're outselling Wayne Enterprises," one reporter said. "Any comment?"

"I'm outselling them two to one!" Edward replied haughtily.

Another raised a finger. "The *Times* has named you Bachelor of the Year, Mr. Nygma. What do you have to say?"

Edward smiled. "You might want to ask Bruce Wayne about that."

He led the way across the floor to Bruce and Chase. "So glad you could come," he greeted them.

"Congratulations, Edward," Bruce said. "Nice suit."

Edward let the remark pass. "The press were just wondering what it feels like to be outsold, outclassed, outcoiffed, outcoutured, and generally outdone in every way." His eyes lit up as he noticed Chase for the first time and appraised her cool beauty. He kissed her hand theatrically as she introduced herself. Then he turned to Bruce again. "How humiliating my success must be for you. When all this could have been ours together!"

Edward grasped Chase's hand. "Shall we dance?" he asked, and whisked her away into the throng. Slightly irritated, Bruce wandered over to one of the booths and pulled open the curtain. Empty, except for a sudden greenish glow.

"Naughty, naughty! Looking for something?"

Bruce started guiltily as the girl called Sugar waved a finger at him in mock admonition. "How to turn it off, actually."

Sugar pressed a button and the booth's power pack ejected into her hand. Smiling his thanks, Bruce entered the booth — and failed to see Sugar catch the dancing Edward's attention. He nodded briefly but emphatically, and Sugar quickly replaced the power pack in its holder.

Inside, there was a bright green flash. Bruce seemed to find himself standing in the center of a lush tropical jungle. Gaily colored birds screeched, and monkeys chattered high above him. Sunlight was filtering down in long, distinct beams that pierced the high jungle canopy and danced on the ferns around him.

He knew it wasn't real, of course, but he had to keep reminding himself of that fact. The whole scene was so ultrarealistic, so completely engrossing, that he foresaw distinct problems with 3-D junkies in the future.

In reality, he was standing in an empty booth staring at a jungle scene on a TV screen, enveloped in its greenish glow. Perched atop the set rested the latest Box . . . and now, as Bruce stood entranced, a tiny white beam blazed out from it, striking him in the center of the forehead.

In the control station back on Claw Island, a tiny status panel flashed as it was activated. On its screen, a schematic of a human brain appeared. Beneath tiny running columns of data analysis, a graphic flashed: Wayne, Bruce.

Edward Nygma's new-generation Box took the entire concept a whole stage further. Now, as well as feeding off the neural energy of any person who used his Box, he could also make a complete computer simulation of their brain. And hence their mind.

Out on the dance floor Edward whirled Chase round, happier than he'd ever been. A billionaire — a genius — and now, he'd decided, he was going to have the most beautiful girl in Gotham, too. He had it made!

Suddenly the lights went out and gunfire burst above the startled revelers' heads.

Two-Face and his thugs blocked every entrance.

Chapter 11

The tropical jungle had vanished and Bruce found himself back in the darkened booth. Disoriented, he felt his way to the exit, and pulled up short as a second burst of bullets peppered the wall behind him.

"This is an old-fashioned, low-tech stickup," Two-Face yelled, and Bruce took the opportunity to slip back into the shadows. "Jewelry, cash, watches, plastic, high-end cellular phones."

A woman screamed as his thugs moved into the frightened mass of partygoers. "Hand everything over nice and easy and nobody gets hurt!"

Bruce kept low, made his way round the walls, keeping to the inky shadows. He backed out through an unwatched fire exit, slid down to the alleyway outside, and hit the ground running.

"Emergency, Alfred!" he rasped, wrenching open the Bentley's rear door. The car was parked only a street away, Alfred using the waiting time to read a book.

The door safely secured behind him, Bruce threw open a secret panel in the back, then reached in to bring out a Bat-suit.

Inside, the double-edged villain's thugs were circulating, yanking jewels from necks and ears, pulling watches and gold bracelets from wrists, filling their sacks with their spoils. Standing on a balcony, Dick stared hard at his hated enemy, then slipped away toward the access stairs.

Lips pursed, Edward Nygma strode up, pushed his way through Two-Face's personal guards, and stuck his face close to that of his partner-in-crime. "You're ruining my party! Are you insane? Actually, considering your present behavior, I withdraw the question!"

There was a sneer on Two-Face's lips. "We're sick of waiting for you to deliver Batman, Riddle-boy!"

Edward shook his head. "Have patience, bifurcated one!"

"Our patience is snapped!" Two-Face told him. "We want him dead . . . and nothing brings out the Bat like a little mayhem and murder!"

There was a loud crash of breaking glass and, gripping his Batline, Batman swung in through the window like some avenging angel of the night. His feet lashed out, dropped three thugs before he let go of the wire and twisted to the floor, and moved into a karate kick that took a gunman in the jaw and dropped him without a sound.

Edward grinned at Two-Face. "Your entrance was good, Harv. His was better. What's the difference? Showmanship!"

Two-Face pushed his partner impatiently away, looking for a clean shot at his nemesis as Batman showed several more thugs just why he was regarded as the best unarmed fighter in the world.

Two-Face loosed a couple of wild shots, shattering an ice sculpture that had taken some poor chef several days to carve. Glasses splintered into shards, and people dived for the floor, screaming.

A street away, Dick Grayson stuck his head through the Bentley window. "Emergency, Alfred!"

Alfred sighed. "I'm sure to be fired for this." He reached beneath the seat and brought something out. "Oh well. Perhaps I can get a job at Buckingham Palace. I always liked the Queen."

A huge, lumbering thug had Chase pinned to a wall, his hand on the string of pearls she wore round her neck. The man grunted as he felt a hand on his shoulder, heard a voice with the texture of broken glass: "Excuse me."

Then Batman head-butted him and he went down in an untidy heap.

Seizing advantage of his closeness, Chase suddenly gripped Batman's arm. "My place," she hissed. "Midnight!"

Annoyed, Batman pulled away. This was no time for romantic games! He made a short run, jumped up onto a table, and dived full-length into another bunch of goons, sending them sprawling to the floor. His gas-pistol was in his hand, spraying a cloud of colorful mist in their faces. The knockout gas acted almost instantaneously and would keep them out for hours. He, of course, wore nose filters.

Two-Face heard the sound of sirens outside. "Okay, boys!" he called out. "Phase two!"

He and several of his personal guards ran into the express elevator, leaving the others to deal with Batman — or, at least, to slow his pursuit. Batman was only seconds behind them, but already the elevator car was speeding downward. He sprinted out onto the balcony and saw Two-Face and his men emerge from the side exit.

Construction work was under way at the side of the hotel, and Batman watched as Two-Face and the others disappeared down an open manhole in the center of the site. Barely pausing to consider, Batman leaped down after them.

In the abandoned subway station that lay under the

street, Two-Face looked up to see the descending shadow of the Bat block the moonlight streaming through the manhole. "Welcome our guest, boys!"

The thugs quickly hoisted into place a translucent red plastic pipe, an industrial air-conditioning tube whose diameter exactly matched that of the manhole. It snaked across the long-deserted platform and the fragmented scaffolding that lay there, into an abandoned side tunnel. Two-Face had been gambling on the Dark Knight's showing up. The plan he'd devised was foolproof.

Batman dropped down through the manhole — and directly into the tube. Slithering and sliding, trying in vain to break his fall, he plummeted through the red vinyl toward darkness.

Then his drop came to a sudden end as he smashed with bone-jarring force into a wall.

"Nothing more than a bad case of gas." Two-Face laughed as he spun the creaking wheel of an aging valve set into the crumbling wall.

Near the dazed Batman, the open end of a pipe began to hiss as escaping gas rushed from it.

Two-Face laughed again, took a step back, and pointed a modern grenade launcher toward the tunnel. "The Bat hath flown," he quoted to his uncomprehending thugs. "Now shall be done a deed of dreadful note."

His thugs dived for cover as he fired. The grenade flew into the tunnel and slammed into the gas main. There was a second of awful silence, like the calm before a thunderstorm strikes, and then an ear-shattering explosion seared the darkness.

A flaming white fireball spun toward Batman at blinding speed. In one swift movement he swirled his cape so that it enclosed his entire body, an instant before he was engulfed in a world of flame.

Smoke billowed from the tunnel, debris and residual flame everywhere. Two-Face stood staring at the inferno, then burst into song: "We are the champions, my friend! We'll keep on fighting to the —"

His smirk vanished like a light going out as a shape rose, phoenixlike, out of the flames. Batman's cape boasted a fire-retardant lining; he'd thought he was going to cook with the heat in there, but he wasn't even singed.

Consumed with rage, Two-Face blasted a section of the wall's support scaffolding and began to wrench it off with crazed fury. "Blast you! Why won't you just die?" In a final surge of maniacal strength, he pulled it free. Its ancient supports gone, the scaffolding began to crack and fall.

Part of the ceiling gave way, and sand and debris from the tunnel lining poured through the ruptured brickwork like water gushing from a tap. Batman raised an arm to ward off a heavy metal girder, then Two-Face lost sight of him in a cloud of stinging dust.

It parted, and Two-Face rejoiced as he saw his old enemy struggling under a rain of sand and rock. Plaster and rubble fell ever more furiously, burying him in the avalanche. Batman's hands scrabbled for purchase but found none. Suddenly the ground beneath his feet gave, and he tumbled down to find himself being sucked into a fast-filling pit of sand and rock. He sent a Batarang spinning upward — but the roof was gone, and there was nothing there for it to grip.

The rubble was up to his chest now; he could hardly breathe, let alone move. Then the sand came up over his mouth, touched the bottom of his mask, rose inexorably to cover his eyes, his head . . . until finally he was buried, one hand protruding from the pit like a drowning swimmer's last desperate gesture for help.

Two-Face's eyes filled with childish delight, but he wasn't crazy enough not to know when his own life was threatened. Deep cracks split the floor in front of him as it started to give way, and he backed off judiciously.

"Boys, let's go have us a party!" He was already running for the exit, and they followed him gratefully, anxious to be out of this madness as quickly as possible.

Sand continued to fall with a quiet hiss as the madman's voice drifted back along the tunnel: "Anybody else feel like donuts?"

Chapter 12

From the very start of his crime-fighting crusade, Batman had recognized the possibility — the probability, Alfred would have said — of his own death. He knew that the stunts he pulled, the risks he took every night, couldn't always go right for him. One night, somehow, something would go wrong and he'd be found by police in the morning, cold and stiff, and Gotham would no longer have a protector.

Now, buried beneath tons of sand and rubble, he feared that time had come. He'd taken a deep gulp of air as soon as the sand had reached his mouth, filling his lungs so he'd last as long as possible. But the sheer quantity of sand, the weight of it on top of him, meant that he could do nothing. He couldn't move, couldn't see, couldn't breathe. Only one gloved hand, protruding inches above the surface, would be the marker for his grave.

Just as the still-trickling sand started to cover even his fingers, a green gauntlet reached down to grab his hand.

Overhead, dangling head down from a rope in an aerialist's maneuver, Dick Grayson secured his grip and started to heave. He wore his Flying Grayson costume, a black mask covering enough of his face for it to be an effective disguise. Gritting his teeth, sweating with the strain, he exerted all his strength. Nothing happened.

Dick strained again, pulling as hard as he could.

Seconds later, Batman's face broke the surface of the sand. Using the leverage of his body on the rope to pull harder, Dick heaved again, and Batman began to rise, free.

The two stood facing each other, hands still clasped, in silence.

Less than half an hour later, as Alfred bandaged his wounds in the cool shadows of the Batcave, Bruce rebuked the teenager. "What the devil did you think you were doing?"

Dick shook his head. "You have a real gratitude problem, you know that, Bruce?" He considered. "I need a name. Batboy? Nightwing? What's a good sidekick name?"

"How about Richard Grayson, college student?" Bruce

snapped, as Alfred pinned the bandage to his shoulder. "This conversation is over!"

Dick shook his head again. "I saved your life, Bruce. You owe me. I'm joining up," he went on, supremely confident.

Bruce was having none of it. "You're totally out of control. You're going to get yourself killed!"

"I'm going to be your partner," the boy assured him. "Whenever the call comes, I'll know. Whenever you go out at night, I'll be watching. And wherever there's Batman, I'll be right behind him. How are you going to stop me?"

Bruce's gaze held Dick's. "I can stop you," he said simply, and Dick knew it was true. Angrily, he turned away and stormed out of the cave. Bruce stared after him, rubbed his eyes, and sighed.

"And you're encouraging him!" he said accusingly to Alfred.

The butler shrugged. "Sir, young men with a mind for revenge need little encouragement. They need guidance."

A picture of Batman flashed on one of the monitor screens, and Bruce turned his attention to it. He'd programmed his computers to constantly scan all radio and TV broadcasts, as well as police messages, for mention of his alter ego.

A guest on a late-night talk show was trashing the vigilante. "Batman is a magnet for so-called super villains," he was saying, presumably in an attempt to beef up his own flagging career. "Only when Batman hangs up cape and cowl will Gotham be spared these evildoers' violent vendettas."

Bruce's mouth set in a grim line as he moved to turn the sound down. He thought deep for a moment, then: "Are they right, Alfred?" he asked the old man. "Is it time for Batman to retire?" He paused, and almost as if speaking to himself added: "Why do I keep doing this?"

"Your parents are avenged. The Wayne Foundation contributes a fortune to anticrime programs. Police handle much of the villainy." The older man shrugged. "Why indeed do you keep doing it?"

Bruce didn't have an answer. "Chase talks about Batman as if he were a curse, not a choice. What frightened me the night of my parents' wake? The bat?" He looked around him at the huge cave and its vast array of crime-fighting equipment. "Did I create all this just because a little boy was scared of a monster in the dark? I thought I became Batman to fight crime. . . . But maybe I became Batman to fight the fear."

"And instead you *became* the fear," Alfred said quietly.

Bruce went on as if he hadn't heard. "If I quit, would Two-Face end his crusade? Could I leave the shadows? To spare Dick. To have a life. Friends. Family."

He paused for a moment, and when he spoke again his voice was pained. "I know now I've never been in love before. But Chase loves Batman — not Bruce Wayne."

"Go tell her," Alfred said straightforwardly, always one for the simplest solution. "Tell her how you feel."

Bruce just looked more troubled. "How? As Batman, knowing that she wants me? Or as Bruce, and hope . . . ?" He let his voice fade, then: "Who am I, Alfred? I don't think I know anymore."

Moonlight stole in through the bedroom window. Chase Meridian lay asleep, deep in dreams.

A shadow fell across her face, lingered a moment, and she stirred. Her eyes opened and she gasped to see the silhouette of Batman standing in the open French doors.

Sliding out of bed, she pulled her pale robe around her and moved to stand beside him. Her finger lightly traced the line of his mask, then his arms went round her and they kissed.

Chase broke away first with a nervous little laugh. "I'm sorry. I just can't believe it. I've imagined this moment since I first saw you. You and I together . . ."

She walked back across the room, away from him. "And now I have you, and . . ." She shook her head, rueful. "I guess a girl has to grow up sometime. You see, I . . . I've met someone else. He's not . . . you. But . . . I hope you can understand."

Batman's eyes hadn't left her since his arrival. Now, as his glance darted round the room, he saw that her Batman photos had been replaced — with newspaper clippings on Bruce Wayne.

Batman smiled, mysteriously, then without another word he was over the balcony and gone, a shadow blending into the darker shadows of the Gotham night.

On his electronic throne in the Claw Island control center, Riddler indulged himself with more stolen neural power. Rivulets of energy rippled and danced under his forehead. The neural fix had turned almost into a necessity for him, the resulting boost to his intelligence the equivalent of the excited rush a drug addict was meant to feel.

He hit a button, and the bank of monitor screens that flanked him burst into life. All bore a single image: Chase Meridian. He hadn't been able to keep his thoughts off her since that magic moment when, as Edward Nygma, he'd held her close and they'd danced together. He stared hard at the image his Box had secretly captured, as if by mere willpower he could conjure up her real presence.

But it was Two-Face who entered the chamber, swaggering and full of himself. "Our belfry is finally free of bats!" he said gleefully. "An end to late-night raids by the man in rubber! No more troublesome explosions of violence from the winged ferret! Ding dang dong, the annoying Bat is dead!"

His scarred side caught the light, and his smile was immediately replaced by a sneer. "So why do we need you?"

he demanded, grabbing the Riddler harshly by the throat. "We're going to be the smartest in Gotham City. We're taking the empire for ourselves! Time's up, laughing boy."

"Bad news, pals," Riddler rasped, the grin never leaving his face. "The Bat lives!"

He gestured to the desk where a late-edition newspaper lay. BATMAN SURVIVES SUBWAY SABOTAGE, its headline blared, seeming to mock Two-Face, making him even angrier. He threw back his head and screamed, a lunatic howl that sent shivers running up the Riddler's spine.

"Someone's going to die!" Two-Face vowed, drawing his gun and pointing it at Riddler's head.

Not for the first time, Edward Nygma found himself wondering if perhaps he'd made the wrong choice of partner. But the game wasn't played out yet. "Kill me? Okay, go ahead. Take the empire." Two-Face watched, puzzled, as Riddler took his own head in both hands. "Tell you what, old pals, I'll even kill me for you!"

Riddler began to slam his head against the desktop, the sound loud and ugly in the cool high-tech chamber. "Too . . . bad . . ." He punctuated every word with another slam. ". . . about . . . Batman."

Two-Face grabbed him, stopping the next jerk forward. "What about Batman?"

Riddler smoothed his hair, his expression smug. "What if you could know a man's mind? Would you not then own that man?" He hit the same switch that had called up Chase's image, which was replaced on the screen by film of Bruce Wayne stepping into the simulation booth at the party. "My new Box knows a new trick. Not only does it drain the brain . . . it makes a map of the mind."

Another touch of the button and the screens changed again, now showing a turning schematic of a human brain, alive with neural lightning. "Would you like to see what my old friend Bruce has in his head?" Riddler asked.

Without waiting for a reply, he jiggled a dial. Another image pulled free from the diagram of Bruce's brain. A trapped bat, fierce and monstrous, wings spread and fangs bared. The same bat Bruce had seen time and time again in his sweat-drenched nightmares.

"Riddle me this, Two-Face: What kind of man has bats on the brain?" Two-Face stared at him as what he was saying sank home. Riddler grinned. "Go ahead. You can say it."

"Riddler," Two-Face said admiringly, "you are a genius!"

Dick Grayson felt as if he'd been punched in the stomach. Hard.

"What do you mean — it's over?" he asked.

He and Bruce were in the Batcave, where Bruce had called him saying he had to make an important announcement. Dick's hopes had run away with him. He'd seen himself in the new costume he'd designed, swinging through the Gotham night. He'd even come up with the

106

name he'd use. Robin. What Dad had called him when he saved Chris's life.

But as he listened to Bruce's flat tones, all his hopes were dashed. "You were right, Dick. As long as there's a Batman, you'll be behind him. But without Batman, you'll never track Two-Face down. Never." He took a deep breath, then said the words he'd never thought would pass his lips: "From this night on, Batman is no more."

Bruce stretched out a hand to throw a switch, and the cave plunged into darkness.

"But — you can't quit," Dick protested. "There are monsters out there! Batman has to protect the innocent!"

"I've spent my life protecting people I've never met, faces I'll never see," Bruce said quietly. "Well, the innocent aren't faceless anymore. If I let you lose yourself to a life of revenge, all I've lived for will have been for nothing. Batman has to vanish so you can live . . . maybe so we all can."

"My dad always said every man goes his own way," Dick blustered. "My way leads to Two-Face!"

"And when you find him . . . what then?" Bruce's gaze was piercing, and Dick looked away, a little shamed. "Exactly," Bruce went on. "You'll kill him. And then you'll be lost. Like me." His voice became softer. "You have to let this go, Dick. Get on with your life. Trust me. I'm your friend —"

"I don't need a friend!" Dick almost cursed. "I need a partner. Two-Face has to pay! Please, Batman! . . ."

"Batman is no more," Bruce said again, a note of chill finality in his voice. He walked toward the steps that led up to the secret door. "Chase is coming for dinner. Come upstairs. We'll talk."

But Dick made no move to follow. He just stood there hunched up into himself, wishing the cool, soothing darkness could swallow him forever.

Chapter 13

ive!" The voice that spoke from behind the horrific skeleton face was suitably deep and spooky. The monster next to him grinned and nudged the werewolf in the side. "Trick or treat!" they all howled together.

Alfred had seen them coming on the manor's closed-circuit security monitor and was already waiting with bags of candy and fruit. Truth to tell, he'd quite forgotten it was Halloween, what with everything that was going on in his life.

He sighed as he went back inside and closed the door.

The children ran laughing down the drive. The Wayne place was a hassle to get to, but the old butler always made it more than worth the trick-or-treaters' while. They quieted when they saw a van parked there, the ways kids automatically do when adults are around. And when a gloved hand at the end of an emerald-green arm appeared from the van, beckoning them over, they didn't think twice.

In the Batcave, a grave Dick Grayson opened the costume vault. He passed over the many and various Batman costumes, each one designed for use in a different crime-fighting circumstance, until he came to the one he'd made and stowed there, so sure that Batman was going to ask him to be his partner. Adapted from his Flying Graysons gear, it was green and yellow with a splash of red on the vest.

He gave the costume a last look, then stuffed it in his bag. He went over to the vehicle bay, wheeled out his motorcycle, and started to push it down the long rock tunnel to the dirt road.

Robin, he thought bitterly, *is one bird that will never fly!*

The flames from the roaring fire in the living room flickered across Bruce's and Chase's faces. They sat close to each other, so close that Bruce's heart thumped madly in his chest.

"I need to tell you something," he began, at exactly the same moment as Chase said: "I have something to tell you."

Both broke off, laughing.

"What I wanted to say —" Bruce tried again, just as Chase told him: "Something happened last —"

Again they laughed, before Bruce deferred to her. "Bruce, since I met you, I . . ." She hesitated, shaking her head. "Blast! Why am I so nervous?"

She reached for her glass of wine, her wrist brushing against a vase and knocking it over. Two red roses fell to the floor. About to apologize, she turned back to Bruce — to see that his eyes were far away, his thoughts back in the distant past.

As if in a dream, he saw roses hit the alley floor. His mother falls. Blood.

"It's happening again," he breathed. "Flashes of my parents' death!"

Chase was at once beside him. "Your memories are trying to break through. Let them come," she coaxed.

"I'm not sure I want to remember."

She squeezed his arm, reassuring. "You braved those thugs at the circus. You braved your parents' death. You can brave the past, Bruce."

There was a slight pause, then Bruce closed his eyes and leaned back. "My parents' coffins are in the library. There's a book on my father's desk. I'm opening the book.

Reading. Then I'm running out into the storm, the book in my hands. I'm screaming, but I can't hear myself over the pounding rain. I'm falling into a hole . . ."

"What hurts so much?" Chase asked. "What does the book say?"

"My father's book. His diary." It was as if he'd been transported back over the years, the book on the desk before him, the smell he would always love, of antique leather bindings. A glance at the coffins. Could these waxy figures, like mannequins that had never been alive, really be his parents? Tears in his eyes, he touches the book, and a wind from nowhere blows the pages open.

"October thirty-first," he told Chase. "Halloween. The last entry . . . the night they died." He took a deep breath, as if to calm himself before the memory flooded back. "'Bruce insists on seeing a movie tonight,'" he said aloud, as if reading from the diary now.

He opened his eyes, and looked miserably at Chase. "I insisted. I made them go out. I made them take me to the movie — to that theater. To that alley." He swallowed a lump in his throat. "It was my fault, Chase. I killed them!"

Past and present resolved around him, and the room came back to normal. "After I read it," he went on bleakly, "I grabbed the book and ran out into the storm. But I couldn't outrun the pain. I tripped, fell into a sinkhole . . ."

He broke off as a sudden realization struck him. "Not the bat?" he said, puzzled.

"What?" Chase didn't understand.

"I thought it was the bat that scared me that night," he explained. "The bat that changed my life. But it wasn't." He tapped himself on the chest, above the heart. "This is the monster I grew strong and fierce to defeat. The demon I've spent my life fighting. My own guilt. The fear that I killed my own parents."

Chase put an arm around him, comforting. "You were a child, Bruce. You weren't responsible."

Her face was close to his, so close she could feel his breath on her cheek. Her lips parted, came down softly on his, and they kissed properly for the first time.

The doorbell rang.

In the hallway, Alfred saw the same masked faces as before. "Trick or treat?" a plaintive voice cried.

Thinking that perhaps they were making too much of a good thing, Alfred took his candy sack and opened the door.

His jaw dropped as Two-Face, Riddler, and an assortment of thugs confronted him.

"Trick," Riddler laughed, bringing his cane down hard on the butler's head. Thugs caught the collapsing body, bundled it into a closet, and bolted the door.

Bruce heard footsteps outside the dining room, and knew at once it wasn't Alfred. As both doorways were flung open and armed thugs swarmed in, Bruce was already moving. He grabbed the silver serving tray and flipped a pot of boiling coffee over the first man. He swung the platter and brought it down on the second mook's head with an echoing clang.

Before the thugs from the other end could reach them, he'd grabbed Chase's hand and pulled her from the room.

They raced along the hallway, the gang in pursuit. Bruce pulled over a couple of heavy statues as he passed, buying them a few more precious seconds as the lead pursuer tripped and fell.

Using the scanner in the head of his cane — another of his enhanced brain's inventions — the Riddler located the secret entry to the Batcave. The door swung open to his touch, and he went gleefully through.

He sauntered down into the cave and found the lights; his eyes widened as its treasures spread out before him. Bruce Wayne had been a very busy boy indeed! From his pouch the Riddler produced several tiny green bombs, each shaped like a bat. He wound one up, its head screeching with every twist of the neck.

The first bomb flew into the wall of video screens and exploded, sending glass and debris everywhere. Sparks and fizzes marked the ends of sheared-off power cables. The costume vault and the crime lab quickly followed, the miniaturized bombs packing all the force of several pounds of TNT.

Smirking, pleased with his destructive handiwork, Riddler wound the last bomb as he turned to mount the stairs again. He tossed it hard, and it fell with a clatter into the cockpit of the Batmobile, parked in the vehicle bay.

With a dull roar and a flash of fiery red, the gleaming black machine exploded.

The lump on Alfred's head was swelling rapidly, but the old retainer paid it no heed. Unable to shoulder the closet door open, he activated his wrist videophone. Tones sounded as the autodial raced across the tiny screen: 9 . . . 1 . . . 1.

Bruce and Chase fled up the wide, ornate staircase together, the thugs mere steps behind. One dived and grabbed a handful of Chase's dress. Bruce thought she was going to go down, but she lashed out with a foot and caught the man squarely, sending him toppling back down the stairs.

Then they were at a small landing near the top. Bruce pulled up beside the twin suits of genuine medieval armor that stood to the side. "Go!" he yelled, and Chase ran on as he sent the heavy metal tumbling and crashing down on top of their attackers. He paused long enough to take out another with a savage spinning karate kick, then sprinted after Chase up to the landing at the top.

Two-Face stood on the floor below. His coin spun in his

hand; it landed evil side up. He raised his gun coolly, deliberately, and squeezed off a shot at Bruce's head. His aim was off, and Bruce was only grazed. But he fell to the stairs, senses reeling, then collapsed backward and started to roll.

Chase screamed — and screamed again as thugs rushed up to grab her.

Bruce landed on the floor below and lay unmoving at Two-Face's feet. "You sure know how to throw a party, Brucie-boy!" the villain laughed. He cocked the gun, about to shoot at point-blank range, but Riddler rushed up and pulled him back.

"No killing," he reminded his partner. "We wreck everything he holds dear, leave him broken, knowing that his secret is out, and death will surely come!"

"Right." Two-Face nodded, and turned away as the sound of approaching sirens drifted in from outside. The Riddler paused long enough to drop another riddle before they fled. "We're five little items of an everyday sort," the card read. "You'll find us all in a tennis court."

He laughed out loud as he saw Two-Face's men carry out a screaming Chase. Yes, everything was perfect in this best of all possible worlds.

Chapter 14

ommissioner Gordon stood on the flat roof of Police HQ, next to the huge searchlight that cast the Bat-Signal up into the Gotham night. For the hundredth time, he wondered where Batman was. He always showed when the signal was up. Maybe . . . Jim Gordon reined back the thought.

Only two things would keep Batman away: injury or . . . worse.

The voices seemed to come from far away. "The injuries are relatively minor. The shot did cause a concussion, though. Watch for headaches — memory lapses — odd behavior. I'll check back in a couple of days."

Bruce opened his eyes in time to see Alfred usher the

doctor out of the bedroom. Bruce was lying in bed, his head bandaged; the wound throbbed painfully.

"Are you all right?" Alfred asked in concern as Bruce sat up.

"As well as can be expected. Well enough to take the bad news."

Alfred wrinkled his face apologetically. "Master Dick has run away. Two-Face and Riddler have taken Doctor Meridian. And I'm afraid they found the cave, sir. It's been destroyed."

Bruce looked hard at the butler. "Cave?" he asked, genuine puzzlement in his voice. "What cave?"

The cave that had once been a cathedral to crimefighting was now in ruins. The Batmobile, the crime lab, nothing was even recognizable for what it had been only hours before.

Bruce looked around it in disbelief, Alfred by his side.

"I remember my life as Bruce Wayne," he said. "But . . . all this. It's like the life of a stranger."

"Perhaps the fall," Alfred murmured. "Amnesia . . ."

Bruce didn't seem to hear him. "There's one other thing. I feel . . . afraid."

Alfred took his arm and looked deep into his eyes. He'd devoted his life to serving this man and the mission he was on, and though it pained him to see Bruce hurt in his role as Batman, it pained him even more to see him like this. "Bruce. Son. You are a kind man. You are a strong man. But in truth you are not the most sane man." He paused, then went on softly: "You gave up being Batman to save a friend. But perhaps you also gave him up because you never really faced why you became the Batman in the first place."

Bruce shuddered. "The cave," he said, and his voice quaked with fear. "I remember the cave. Something chasing me. A demon!"

Alfred put a cool hand on his master's fevered brow. "No demons, son. Your monsters are here, inside you. And until you face them, I fear you will spend your whole life fleeing them."

In his control room at Nygmatech, Riddler sat enthroned, absorbing neural energy. The video screens banked beside him showed a photofile of Bruce Wayne, and the newsreader's voice narrated how the billionaire was continuing to recover from nonspecified head injuries.

"Batman will come for me!" Chase's voice broke in on his mutterings. She was chained to the base of his throne, held captive like a slave, or a dog. But she'd seen enough to have guessed what Riddler was up to, and she knew enough to know it was exceedingly dangerous.

"Your bat's gonna come," Riddler sang. Then, suddenly lethal: "I'm counting on it!"

Chase snorted with derision. "There's a reason we only use a fraction of our brains," she told him. "You're cutting neural pathways faster than your consciousness can incorporate them. You're frying your mind!"

Riddler leaned down, his face thrust close to Chase's. "Spoil the mood, why don't you?" He pulled out a hypodermic syringe filled with green liquid. "Nap time, gorgeous," he grinned, as he plunged it into her arm.

Deep in the Batcave, Bruce stood before a dark, rocky passage. Through here and beyond was an area he'd never really explored, an area he'd kept away from since . . . since that night as a boy when he'd found it. The walls seemed to crowd in on him, sweating granite, a shifting world of sinister shadows.

Biting his lip, Bruce forced himself on into the darkness. The walls around him undulated, moving as if covered in a sheen of water. But it was bats, thousands of them — tens of thousands of them — clinging there, leathery wings rustling.

Perspiration broke out on Bruce's brow, and he felt a cold trickle of fear run slowly down his back. Ahead, diffuse moonlight came in from somewhere above, illuminating a curving rock chamber that was alive with bats.

Bruce moved into the moonlight and looked up — to see the narrow, rocky chute where he fell as a child.

He knelt on the floor, and there before him, worn by years of weather, was his father's diary.

The leather bindings must have been soaked and frozen and baked by the sun hundreds of times over the years, but incredibly, when he lifted it, that well-loved smell of old leather and mold hit his nostrils. His fingers lingered for a moment on his father's name, embossed on the front, before he turned the yellowed, crumbling pages to the very last entry. He could hardly bring himself to read. Was this what he feared most in all the world — final confirmation that it really was his fault his parents had died?

"Bruce insists on seeing a movie tonight . . ." He read the words he'd been able to recall when Chase was quizzing him, and it felt like a knife stabbing him in the heart. He almost put the book down then, the weight of his sin too heavy for him to bear. But he gathered himself, forced his fumbling fingers to turn that final page.

". . . but Martha and I have our hearts set on Zorro, so Bruce's cartoon will have to wait until next week."

The words made no sense the first time he read them. He devoured them again, scarcely daring to believe the hope that welled up in his heart. It wasn't his fault! All these years . . . and it wasn't his fault!

He lifted his face to the moonlight, and tears streamed unashamedly down his cheeks.

Suddenly, there was a movement in the darkness ahead.

A head rose, slits opening to reveal two blood-red eyes. Huge wings spread.

Then the giant monarch bat was airborne, the sound of its flapping wings like thunder in the confined space. Eyes gleaming, fangs bared, it soared toward him.

Bruce stiffened, terror coursing through him. He turned to run, to flee, to get away from here . . .

But no. He fought off the impulse and stood his ground. He'd been running from his fears for a long time, and see where it had got him. Alfred was right — it was time to face what he was afraid of. Resolved, he faced the monster as it soared right up to him.

Then, remarkably, the bat stopped, holding its position, hovering in the air like some giant butterfly from hell.

Those blood-red eyes bored into his.

Bruce raised his arms. *Like wings,* he thought.

Man and bat faced each other in the pale moonlight on the cave floor. On the wall, their shadows seemed to flow and run together, touching, blending, merging into one shimmering white light.

In the main cave, Alfred waited. There was a sudden commotion, and he jumped back as thousands of screaming, screeching bats exploded from the tunnel. Standing among them, almost lost behind the intricate tracery of swooping wings, was the figure of a man.

"Master Bruce?" the old retainer said, uncertain.

"Batman," came the reply. "I'm Batman!"

But there was no Batman to answer the bright signal that lit the sky. Beneath it, Commissioner Jim Gordon was about to give up. There was no chance of his showing now. A heavy weight sat on the commissioner's shoulders as he thought of Gotham City without its Darknight Detective. And almost as bad: Jim would have lost one of his very few true friends.

He moved to the searchlight, taking one last look at the probing signal before he went to shut it off. But his hand froze.

In the air above the signal, a greenish glow was forming, coagulating . . .

Gordon cursed. It was a giant question mark — the symbol of the Riddler!

Chapter 15

We're five little items of an everyday sort. You'll find us all in a tennis court."

Batman and Alfred stood at the ruined control console in the Batcave, the riddles spread out before them. Bruce finished reading the last riddle aloud, and began circling letters in the words "a tennis court."

"Vowels," he explained. "Five vowels in those words."

Alfred nodded in admiration. "Very clever, sir. But what do a clock, a match, chess pawns, and vowels have in common? What do these riddles *mean?*"

Bruce was thoughtful, trying to cover all the angles. "Maybe the answer isn't in the answers, but in the questions. . . ."

Yes, that could be it! "Every riddle has a number in the

question," he went on, jotting down the numbers 13, 1, 8, and 5.

Alfred scratched his head. "I still don't see what they mean, sir."

"What do maniacs always want?" Bruce asked.

"Recognition, of course."

"Precisely. So this number is some kind of calling card."

He stared at the numbers. He added them: 27. Squared them: 16916425. No luck there. He separated them — 13/18/5. Then —

"Of course!" The answer was so obvious, it had been staring him in the face. "Letters of the alphabet!"

13 — M. 18 — R. 5 — E. Alfred still didn't get it. "MRE, sir?"

"How about MR. E," Bruce suggested. "Mystery."

"Aha!" Alfred beamed. "And another name for mystery is . . . Enigma!"

Bruce nodded. "Mr. E — Mr. Edward Nygma. What wasted genius! The video of Stickley's suicide must have been a computer-generated forgery!"

He walked over to the wrecked Batmobile, its once-flowing lines now warped and broken. "Pretty bad, huh?"

"We've repaired worse, sir."

Bruce smiled, touched a button, and smiled even more broadly as hydraulics hissed into action. "Good thing Mr. E didn't know about the cave beneath the cave!"

The entire platform on which they were standing began to descend slowly through a rocky shaft, gradually giving out into an even deeper cave. Water flowed through this one, a dark, heavy river, jagged rocks protruding from its edge. Here, the Batwing and Batboat were stored, completely untouched by the Riddler's assault on the main cave above.

"What now, sir?"

"Claw Island," Bruce told him, stepping down off the platform. "Nygma's headquarters. I'm sure that's where they're keeping Chase." A realization struck him. "The Batman costumes — all destroyed?"

"All except the prototype with the sonar modifications. But you haven't tested it yet."

Bruce's lips curled almost mischievously. "Tonight's a good night."

Minutes later he was wearing the new costume, with its slightly different design and improved Utility Belt features. Across its chest was emblazoned a large Bat emblem.

"What do you suggest, Alfred? By sea or by air?"

But it wasn't Alfred who answered him. Dick's voice cut out of the darkness: "Why not both?"

He stepped out of the shadows into the moonlight, wearing the new costume he'd made. Black cape, yellow on the inside. Red armored vest, green leggings with knee protectors, flexible black boots. He wore his own version of the Utility Belt, and on his chest a small *R* was emblazoned.

"What's the *R* for?" Batman asked.

Dick glanced at Alfred. "Robin," he said simply. "Riddler and Two-Face look a pretty lethal combination. I thought you could use some help."

"Two against two is better odds," Batman conceded. "But your attitude —"

"— has changed," Robin put in. "Whatever happens, I won't kill him." He hesitated, then went on: "A friend taught me that."

"Not just a friend." Bruce extended his hand, and Robin clasped it. "A partner."

Minutes later, the Batwing roared through the rocky passage and the Batboat sped through the turbulent waters below. For the first time ever, the Dynamic Duo were going into action.

Finally, the Riddler's question mark symbol had died away. Jim Gordon gazed out over the glittering cityscape for a last time, hoping beyond hope, then sadly moved to switch off the Bat-Signal. A roar split the night and Gordon stared upward, puzzled. For a moment, it seemed as if the Bat-Signal itself was swooping down toward him.

Then the Batwing burst through the column of light, buzzing low over the roof, dipping a wing to Gordon.

Triumphant, sudden joy singing in his heart, Gordon waved the Batman onward.

As the dark miniplane buzzed away, the Batboat cut across the waters of the harbor, on silent running. At the helm, Robin stood — steering straight for Claw Island.

Chapter 16

In the Riddler's control center, sensors warned the evil twosome they were about to come under attack.

Riddler punched an instruction into the handset for an electronic Battleship game. "A-14," he called.

"Hit!" Two-Face crowed, as out in the harbor a concealed mortar fired, its deadly cargo exploding just behind the Batboat, sending a waterspout shooting high in the sky.

Two-Face moved a battleship, glowing red. "B-12!"

"Hit!" Riddler cried. "And, I might add, my favorite vitamin."

Out in the harbor another explosion rocked the Batboat, sending Robin off-balance. He dived overboard, kicking deep in the water, as a third shell screamed down and blasted the craft to smithereens.

As debris fell through the water around him, Robin

slipped a rebreather into his mouth and struck out for the island.

But Riddler's defenses weren't penetrated yet.

A spear cleaved the water, missing him by inches, leaving a trail of fine bubbles as it sped by. A second followed, and Robin saw a gang of armed frogmen stream from a hidden underwater bunker. The defenses had cost Nygma a fortune — but what did he care? He had a dozen fortunes, and more to take anytime he wanted it. Robin dodged another spear, and wondered miserably if maybe he'd made a bad mistake.

Above, the Batwing soared over the harbor, its infrared camera scanning the water below. Batman had seen the explosion and knew what it meant. He could only pray Dick had got overboard first. If not . . . he blanked the thought with grim determination.

A blip on his infrared screen showed that Dick was alive — and under severe assault.

But before Batman could respond, a laser beam shot out from the top of Nygma's stronghold and seared the night air.

There was no time for evasive action as it neatly sliced through one of the craft's wings.

The Batwing dived nosefirst, hitting the water with enough impact to stun any normal man. But this was Batman, and the interior was well cushioned, and he was

130

strapped into a harness. He absorbed the force of the crash landing, fingers already stabbing out to hit buttons and switches.

And as the Batwing wafted down through the chill waters, a startling transformation took place. The wheel hubs sealed themselves, making the craft watertight. Dark panels grew sleek fins. A rotor whirred into life at the rear. The Batwing was now the Batsub.

Robin's elbow drove into a frogman's face, and the man fell away. But there were too many of them, swarming around and over him. His arms were grabbed, held tightly, and hands wrenched his rebreather away. A knife slashed through the water, and he could see others swimming to join in.

Then the dark shape of the Batsub approached, its forward firing tubes unleashing a man-sized torpedo. Before the men could scatter, the torpedo burst through them — revealing itself as a capeless Batman!

One hand grabbed Robin as he shot by, the other fired a lightweight Batnet that settled over the attackers, entangling them in its meshes.

Batman powered them upward, and Robin gasped air with sweet relief, as they broke the water's surface and he took a deep, gasping gulp. Batman hooked the Batnet cable to a nearby buoy; the police would know where to find the frogmen.

Then they struck out together, heading for the rocky shore of Claw Island.

Batman lagged behind in the shallows to refasten his cape to his armored shoulder plates as Robin left the water.

"Holey rusted metal, Batman!" Robin burst out.

His mentor frowned. "What?"

Robin took a step forward and knelt on the ground. "The ground. It's metal, and it's full of holes. You know, holey."

"This was a refueling station for submarines during the war —" Batman began, but he broke off as an excruciating crunching noise drowned him out. He stared in disbelief as Robin started to rise swiftly into the air. The whole island itself was lifting!

As it reared up high above him, now as high as a five-story building, he could see the "island" for what it was under its thin coat of soil and rock — an absolutely gigantic cylindrical oil tank. Helplessly, Robin clung to the covering of rock as the gargantuan tank rose up.

No way up there, not even for a Batman! His eyes cast quickly around, settling on a rusting metallic access hatch on the side of the huge cylinder. Ripping it off with a shriek of tortured metal, Batman hurled himself inside.

High above, Robin was wondering how he was going to get out of this one, when a voice spoke behind him.

"We flipped a coin to see who got to kill who." Two-Face was crouched there, ready for action, a wicked-looking blade in his right hand. "We got you!"

Chapter 17

Before Robin had time to react, Two-Face leaped and brought him down.

Robin hit the ground painfully, the villain atop him. Once, twice, thrice, Two-Face head-butted him. Robin saw stars, his senses reeling as he tried futilely to shove the heavier man off.

"What's wrong, circus boy?" Two-Face laughed, the knife in his hand glinting in the moonlight. "No Mommy and Daddy to save you?"

With no further warning, the knife stabbed down — straight at Robin's chest. With one last desperate effort the teenager twisted, rolling just far enough to the side for the knife to miss him. With a dull crunch, the blade wedged into the cylinder's rusted metal surface. Cursing, Two-Face tried to haul it out.

The distraction provided all the time Robin needed. He rolled clear, then back-flipped himself onto his feet again. One booted foot lashed out, striking the villain hard in the head.

"For my mother," Robin said, through gritted teeth.

The split-faced killer fell back, dazed — only to be met by a flying front kick that took him under the chin.

Robin's face was grim. "For my father."

The teenager spun, his left leg rising up and out in a perfectly timed karate kick that knocked Two-Face to his knees.

"For Chris."

As the villain tried to get to his feet, Robin's fist shot out to take him in the face.

"And that one's for me."

Two-Face staggered under the blows, lost his footing on the oil tank's curved surface, and rolled down the slope. His fingers raked dirt and stone, trying and failing to find purchase. He tumbled toward the edge of the cylinder, saw the harbor lights reflected in the water far below, and desperately grabbed onto a jagged rock. He hung on for dear life, his feet kicking out wildly over the abyss.

"You're a man after my own heart, son," he called up to Robin, even as the rock he clung to started to slide and pull free under his weight. Yet, incredibly, there was a big grin on his face.

"See you in Hell, kid!" He laughed as he started to take a long, final fall.

Robin really thought he would let the man plunge to his doom. But Bruce's words echoed in his head, and he knew they were true; if he killed Two-Face, it made him no better than a common murderer. If his family's death was to have any meaning at all, it could only be within a solid framework of justice.

Just in time Robin's hand grabbed the murderer, yanked hard, and hoisted him up to safety again.

"I'd rather see you in jail," the boy spat contemptuously.

"The Bat's taught you well. Noble." As Two-Face spoke, his hand stole unobserved to his pocket and pulled out a gun.

"A mistake," he went on, "but definitely noble!"

Robin gazed into the gun barrel, somehow strangely calm as Two-Face cocked the trigger.

Inside the oil tank, a world of spinning, glowing question marks filled the bottomless void. Ignoring them, Batman sent a Batarang curling high to secure itself to the giant steel grating that was the container's ceiling. Attaching the cable to the small winch on his belt, he was raised quickly into the air as it reeled him in.

But even as he rose toward it, well-oiled mechanics slid into play. The grate began to descend, the question marks disappearing and fading away under the darkness that it cast.

136

Batman changed his grip and spun on the wire so that he was rising upside down, his feet racing toward the plummeting grate. He slapped a switch on his Utility Belt and miniaturized thrusters powered into life, rocketing him upward even faster. Batman braced himself.

Impact! As his feet slammed into the grate, it flipped over like a giant pie pan. Letting go and detaching himself from his line, Batman cut his thrusters and tumbled head over heels in midair. His hands reached out to grab the rungs of an old iron ladder set into the cylinder wall.

He hung there for a moment, looking down to watch the huge, dislodged grate splash into the waters below. He took a deep breath, then pulled himself through a rusted hatch.

The Riddler sat on his throne, a huge antenna shooting up into the night sky behind him through a round hole in the overhead dome. A ring of pulsing light encircled him, feeding him ever more brainpower.

Batman quietly entered the control room, coming in on Riddler's blind side. He frowned. Riddler had changed. His hair had been sculpted and cut into the shape of a large question mark, and instead of Edward Nygma's lanky, awkward body, his muscles now bulged like a steroid-pumped bodybuilder's.

The throne swiveled, bringing the two enemies face to face, thwarting Batman's slim hope of sneaking up on him.

The villain's eyes gleamed insanely. "Riddle me this, riddle me that — who's afraid of the big, black Bat?"

"No more tricks, Edward," Batman said quietly, hoping to appeal to any decency Nygma had left. "Release Chase. This is between you and me."

"And me and me!" A second figure stepped out from behind Riddler into the light. Two-Face!

One look at the antenna and the contents of the room had been enough for Batman to guess the truth. "The Box does more than enhance neural energy," he said accusingly. "You've been sucking Gotham's brain waves!" He glanced over the bank of monitor screens, on which endless schematics of human brains flickered. He remembered the disorientation he'd felt in the booth at the Nygma party. "You've devised a way to map the brain — to read men's minds!"

Riddler shook his head in mock appreciation. "Oh, Bruce, you are clever — but not nearly clever enough! My Box will sit on every TV in the world, mapping brains. Giving me credit card numbers, bank codes, vault combinations. No secret is safe from my watchful electronic eye!"

The madness in his voice became more pronounced. "I will rule the planet! For if knowledge is power, then tremble, world! Edward Nygma has become a god!"

He broke off, turning to Two-Face. "Was that over the top, Harv? I can never tell." Not waiting for his partner's reply, he turned back to Batman. "By the way, B-man — I got your number!"

Every screen lit up with an image of Batman, quickly replaced by images of Bruce. Then the two superimposed. There could be no doubt that they were two aspects of the same man.

"I've seen your mind, freak. Yours is the greatest riddle of all." Riddler's voice was cold and cruel. "Can Bruce Wayne and Batman ever truly coexist?"

Batman didn't flinch, though Riddler's question cut right to the heart of the troubles that had plagued him. Perhaps, before tonight, he'd have answered no. But things were different now.

Riddler twisted the heads on the throne's Thinker armrests, and suddenly his muscular physique split in half. It was simply a solid, formfitting bodysuit. From within stepped Edward Nygma, wearing a skintight leotard festooned with question marks.

"I know who I really am," he said to Batman. "Let's help you decide once and for all exactly who *you* really are. Behind curtain number one . . ."

The girl known as Sugar appeared at the edge of the room, pointing upward to a curtain-draped cylinder suspended overhead. The curtain rose to reveal Chase within the tube, tied up and unconscious.

". . . the captivating Dr. Chase Meridian." Riddler had reverted to his gameshow host persona. "Chase enjoys hiking, getting her nails done, and foolishly hopes Batman will save her!"

Spice appeared at the other side of the room, gesturing toward another hanging tube. When the curtain rose on this one, it was to reveal the bound and beaten Robin inside.

"And behind curtain number *two*, Batman's one and only partner, folks," Riddler went on. "This acrobat turned orphan likes looking his best despite an endless series of bad hair days. And below our contestants, my personal favorite . . ."

Trapdoors beneath each cylinder sprang open. Far below, Batman could make out jagged rocks and crashing surf.

". . . a watery grave!" Riddler finished theatrically.

Chapter 18

Riddler's finger hovered over a button shaped like a glowing green skull. "A simple touch," he warned, "and five seconds later these two players are gull-feed on the rocks below! Not enough time to save them both. So who will it be? Bruce's love? Or Batman's partner?"

Batman knew there was no way he could reach both in time to save them. All he could do was stretch the game out, try to keep things going until Riddler or Two-Face made a mistake. "You've become a monster, Edward," he said quietly.

Riddler snorted with derision. "No. Just the Riddler. And here's yours: What is without taste or sound, all around, but can't be found?" He laughed briskly, then began to hum the theme from the television quiz show *Jeopardy*.

Batman took a step forward, his mind working overtime. No taste or sound — all around — can't be found? Air? No, it can be found. Darkness? Somehow he doubted it; it just didn't seem to fit. Then what?

Riddler and Two-Face chortled at each other. This time, Batman really was dead! The floor that stretched between them wasn't real; over the crisscross skeleton of steel girders on which Riddler had built his lair, a tiny camera projected a holographic floor.

Batman lifted his foot, about to take another step — then stopped abruptly. "Death," he said, and he could tell from the way their smirks vanished that he was right. "Death is the answer to your riddle. Because there is no way for me to save them or myself. This whole scenario is one giant death trap!"

Riddler blew a raspberry. "I'm sorry, but your answer must be in the form of a question. Thanks anyway for playing!"

His finger descended, about to stab the green skull button.

"Wait!" Batman cried. "I have a riddle for *you*."

"For me?" Riddler rubbed his hands together in gleeful anticipation. "Really? Do tell!"

"I see without seeing. To me, darkness is as clear as daylight. What am I?" Even as he spoke, Batman was preparing himself for action. Muscles tensed. His breathing deepened. His hand moved fractionally closer to his Utility Belt.

142

"Oh please!" Riddler scoffed. "Too easy! You're blind as a bat!"

"Exactly!" Batman palmed his belt and hit the hidden stud that released a high-energy Batarang into his hand. He threw it in one smooth motion, directly at the tall antenna.

The Batarang impacted, and there was a tremendous explosion of sparks as the transceiver overloaded.

Riddler shrieked as neural energy pulsed out of control toward him. "No!" he screamed, but there was no way he could escape the massive bursts of stolen brainpower that flooded into his cranium. His entire head seemed to warp and distort, fluctuating in size, as if his brain were struggling to absorb everything being downloaded into it. It bulged out, skin stretching for a moment over his expanding skull, before snapping back into place, deflated.

"Bummer!" Riddler groaned — and then the room went pitch-black.

Riddler's finger came down heavily on the glowing green button. Immediately Robin and Chase dropped through the floor of their cages and plummeted down through dark space.

Twin metal lids flicked shut over Batman's eyes. Small sonar screens — another yet-untested invention — lit up on the inside of the eyepieces. He saw the phantom hologram floor for what it was, and saw the spiderweb tracery of interconnecting metal beams between the chamber and the crashing ocean below.

A second Batarang spun upward, securing itself to the roof dome. Batman swung out and down, snatching Chase from her deadly plunge and depositing her on a wide girder. No time to make sure she was all right — his sonar screens picked out the figure of the falling Robin.

Batman dived headfirst into the abyss, his line shooting out to snag on a girder as he passed. *You can't fail!* a small voice inside him insisted with dogged determination. *He's your partner! You can't fail him!*

The rocks and white-flecked surf below approached at breakneck speed. It looked certain that Robin's limp body would land among them, to be shredded like a rag doll against their jagged edges.

But Batman caught him, mere feet before he slammed to his death — and at exactly the same moment as the Bat-line snapped taut. He activated the tiny winch, and they were hauled swiftly back up to the girder.

As he rested Robin alongside the groaning Chase, blinding white light suddenly filled his screens. Two-Face had strapped a halogen lamp to his head, its intense beams making Batman's sensors useless.

"All those heroics for nothing!" Two-Face aimed his gun, Batman picked out in the spotlight like some giant insect waiting to be pinned. "No more riddles, no more curtains one and two. Just plain curtains, Batty."

He cocked the trigger as Batman replied: "Haven't you

forgotten something, Harvey? You're always of two minds about everything. You can't kill me unless the coin decides!"

Two-Face presented his handsome side and smiled. "Thank you, Bruce." He pulled his silver coin, the one with the scarred side, from his pocket and flipped it into the air. "Life . . . or death!"

Before he could catch the spinning disk, Batman tossed a Batarang, knocking the coin from his hand.

"No!" Two-Face screamed with rage, snatching blindly for the coin. Losing his balance, arms flailing, he toppled from the beam on which he stood. The rocks and the angry sea rushed up to meet him.

"Help Chase," Batman told the recovering Robin. "I'll be back."

Swiftly, he began to scale the girders. He caught sight of Sugar and Spice fleeing for an exit hatch, but didn't try to stop them. Small fry who could be picked up anytime. Riddler was the important one!

The Riddler was in his control room, on his hands and knees, whimpering as he tried in vain to piece together the charred remains of his equipment.

"Why can't I kill you?" he asked in a small, lost voice. "Now there's a riddle. Not smart enough. Find a way. Fuse the transceiver to . . . what? Can't remember. Too many questions. Why you and not me? Why me? Why? Why? Why?"

There was pity in Batman's eyes as he hauled himself up into the room, stood over the pathetic, scrabbling figure. "I had to save them both, Edward," he explained. "I'm Bruce Wayne *and* I'm Batman. Not because I have to be. Because I choose to be."

Gently, Batman reached a hand to help him to his feet. Edward looked up — but it was no man he saw there. Coming toward him out of the darkness was a hideous, demonic, giant bat.

Edward Nygma covered his head with his hands and began to scream a scream that would last for a very long time.

Epilogue

Edward Nygma has been yelling for hours that he knows the true identity of Batman."

Dr. Burton's words made Chase Meridian shiver as she accompanied him down a corridor toward Arkham Asylum's Maximum Security wing. If Batman's secret ever came out, his career as a crime-fighter would be over like a candle being snuffed. Two-Face's body hadn't been found, but it was almost safe to say he'd been killed by the fall. Only Riddler remained as a threat.

Burton opened the small, barred window to a padded cell, and Chase cautiously stepped up to it. "Edward? It's Chase Meridian. Remember me?"

The cell was lit only by moonlight, streaming in the high, shatterproof window. "How could I forget?" Edward Nygma spoke from the shadows in the corner of the cell.

147

"Dr. Burton tells me you know who Batman is."

A high-pitched giggle. "Yesss! I know!"

"Who is the Batman, Edward?"

There was no response, only a burst of nervous giggling.

"Who is Batman?" Chase tried again. "Please, Edward . . ."

A huge shadow like a bat's appeared on the padded wall, silhouetted in the moonlight. Chase gasped — and then Edward leaped from the shadows, the sleeves of his straitjacket flapping madly . . . like the wings of a bat.

"I am!" he cackled. "I am Batmannnnnnnn!"

Chase came down the asylum's front steps to find Bruce waiting for her by the Bentley.

"He's lost all contact with reality," she told him. "Your secret is safe . . ." She leaned close, went on in a quieter voice: ". . . Batman. Or do I just call you Bats?"

Bruce smiled, and reached into his pocket to bring out the small wicker dream-doll she'd given him. It seemed so long ago. He handed it to her.

"I don't need it anymore. My dreams are all good dreams . . . now."

Bruce's arm went round her shoulder and drew her close. He bent his head, and her lips came up to meet his in a long, lingering kiss. The kiss of two people in love.

They broke apart slowly, and Bruce opened the car

door for her to slide in. "Don't work too late," she smiled.

Then Alfred started the engine and they pulled away down the asylum's long drive. In the distance, piercing the lights of Gotham City towering over them, Chase could see the Bat-Signal.

"Does it ever end, Alfred?" she asked softly.

In the driver's seat, Alfred Pennyworth turned his mouth up in a wry smile. "No, miss. Not in this lifetime."

Later, a lone silhouette stood high on the edge of a gargoyled building. Beneath him, Gotham spread like a twinkling, three-dimensional map. His city. His responsibility.

For as long as he breathed, Batman would keep vigil while the decent folk slept and crime roamed free like an uncaged beast.

But from this night on, that vigil would not be kept alone. A second figure stepped from the shadows, taking his place beside his partner, scanning the streets far below. Twin capes whipped in the cool night breeze.

The muffled pop of a gunshot drifted up from below, and together Batman and Robin dived from their perch, twin guardians of the night.

The darkness seemed to open, accepting them like old friends.

About the Author

ALAN GRANT was born in Bristol, England, in 1949 but spent his first twenty years near Edinburgh, Scotland, where his parents, daughter, both brothers, and their families still live. Leaving school when he was seventeen to pursue a career in accounting/banking, he quickly realized he had made a mistake and switched to publishing. He wanted to work in comics, his first love, but instead worked his way up to editor via a variety of romance publications, learning to write women's romantic fiction in the process and producing a successful run of teenage true confessions. He soon quit editorial work to go freelance and, after returning briefly to college, worked on the British comic book sensation *2000 AD*. For a while he became the Puzzle King of Fleet Street, specializing in cryptic crosswords and giant word search/quiz combos. Soon he started to write his first comic strips and went on to script *Judge Dredd*, among many other titles. He is also the coauthor of a series of children's prose anthologies and publisher of several creator-owned comic titles. Mr. Grant is currently the writer of *Batman: Shadow of the Bat* (a series created especially for him), *Lobo*, and many team-up and crossover titles, including the recently published *Batman/Spawn: War Devil*. Other titles he's written for DC include *Batman, Detective Comics, Batman/Judge Dredd, L.E.G.I.O.N.*, and *The Demon*. He has also written *The Incredible Hulk, The Punisher,* and *Robocop,* among other titles, for Marvel Comics. His most recent novel for young readers, *Batman: Knightfall & Beyond,* was a bestseller for Bantam Books. Alan Grant lives and works in a converted twelfth-century church near Colchester, England, with his wife and guardian angel Sue.